Andrew Powell is a family law barrister at 4 Paper Buildings, specialising in surrogacy, the international movement of children, adoption, public law children work and court of protection. He is ranked in the Legal 500 and Chambers and Partners and acknowledged for his expertise in surrogacy law.

Andrew is member of the Family Law Bar Association, The Association of Lawyers for Children, Resolution and is an associate member of the American Bar Association (Family Law Section).

A Practical Guide to the Law in Relation to Surrogacy

A Practical Guide to the Law in Relation to Surrogacy

Andrew Powell
Barrister
4 Paper Buildings, London

Law Brief Publishing

© Andrew Powell

All rights reserved. No part of this publication may be reproduced, stored in a retrieval system, or transmitted, in any form or by any means, electronic, mechanical, photocopying, recording or otherwise, without the prior permission of the publisher.

Excerpts from judgments and statutes are Crown copyright. Any Crown Copyright material is reproduced with the permission of the Controller of OPSI and the Queen's Printer for Scotland. Some quotations including the Form A101A are licensed under the terms of the Open Government Licence (http://www.nationalarchives.gov.uk/doc/open-government-licence/version/3).

Cover image © iStockphoto.com/Tinpixels

The information in this book was believed to be correct at the time of writing. All content is for information purposes only and is not intended as legal advice. No liability is accepted by either the publisher or author for any errors or omissions (whether negligent or not) that it may contain. Professional advice should always be obtained before applying any information to particular circumstances.

Published 2020 by Law Brief Publishing, an imprint of Law Brief Publishing Ltd
30 The Parks
Minehead
Somerset
TA24 8BT

www.lawbriefpublishing.com

Paperback: 978-1-912687-49-7

To all of my family and friends, thank you for your unwavering support.

PREFACE

This book is intended to assist family law practitioners and individuals who seek to gain a better understanding of the law related to surrogacy in England and Wales.

In the last 5 years alone, the number of family law cases concerning aspects of the Human Fertilisation and Embryology Act 2008 has increased significantly. In respect surrogacy, the most recent statistics published by the Ministry of Justice in June 2020 showed that in 2012, 184 parental orders were made in England and Wales, compared to 374 and 440 in 2018 and 2019 respectively.

This increase has brought an expectation from both lay clients and the bench that all family practitioners should have a grounding of the fundamental concepts and relevant legal principles concerning not just surrogacy, but human fertilisation and embryology legislation generally. The law on this area is ever changing, with the Law Commission likely to make proposals for significant legislative reform in the next few years, and therefore the law as set out in this book is current as at 1 October 2020.

Finally, it would be remiss of me not to acknowledge and thank specialist fertility and family law community who have welcomed me into this niche area of work, without whom this book really couldn't exist.

Andrew Powell
October 2020

CONTENTS

Chapter One	Introduction	1
Chapter Two	What Is Surrogacy?	5
Chapter Three	Legal Parenthood and Parental Responsibility	15
Chapter Four	Parental Orders and the Parental Order Criteria	25
Chapter Five	Welfare	79
Chapter Six	Parental Order Reporter and Their Duties	93
Chapter Seven	The Parental Order Application Process	101
Chapter Eight	What Happens When the Criteria for a Parental Order Is Not Met?	121
Chapter Nine	Concluding Comments	141

CHAPTER ONE
INTRODUCTION

1. The concept of 'the family' in English family law is a dynamic and ever-changing one. As family structures have changed, and medical advancements have paved the way for assisted reproduction and surrogacy, English law has adapted to redefine the ever-widening parameters of what constitutes a family.

2. As one High Court Judge observed in a 2015 judgment: Family courtrooms have become *"the vanguard of change in life and society. Where there are changes in medicine or in technology or cultural change, so often they resonate first within the family"*[1]

3. The growing use of surrogacy as a route to parenthood very much represents a change in family life and the way in which the state, through the courts, acknowledges what a family is.

Who is this book for?

4. This book is for lawyers specialising in family law and intended parents wishing to gain an understanding of the statutory framework related to surrogacy. It is also intended to be a practical guide to the process of achieving recognition of parental status between a child born to a surrogacy arrangement and the intended parents.

5. For family lawyers, the importance of understanding the legal framework around surrogacy is one which has come to be expected, particularly in circumstances where surrogacy may

---

1 Per Hayden J in *London Borough of Tower Hamlets v M & Others [2015] EWHC 869 (Fam)* at para [57]

arise in private law litigation unexpectedly. Knowledge therefore of what a parental order is, and the transformative effect that it has is therefore something all family lawyers should have at their fingertips. King J, as she then was, remarked in *JP v LP & Others [2014] EWHC 595 (Fam)* that

> "The application for and granting of parental orders whist not "routine" is no longer the exclusive province of lawyers specialising in reproduction and human embryology law. An understanding of, and ability to make a proper application complying with the provisions of the HFEA 2008, should be as much a part of the skills set of a competent general family practitioner as is a step parent adoption."[2]

Chapter overview

6. In Chapter 2 this book explores the concept of surrogacy, what it is, how it is defined, and the historical context thorough which the current legal framework has emerged.

7. In Chapter 3 key legal concepts of legal parenthood and parental responsibility are examined, and the relevance these legal concepts have to children who are born via surrogacy and their intended parents.

8. Chapter 4, the main chapter, examines the elements contained within the statutory criteria under section 54 of the Human Fertilisation and Embryology Act 2008. (HEFA 2008) that is needed for a court to make a parental order.

9. Chapter 5 shall consider the welfare concept and how that is applied in surrogacy cases. It also takes a critical examination of

---

2 Per King J at para [43]

'life story' work in respect of identity for donor conceived children.

10. Chapter 6 examines the role of the parental order reporter and what their duties are to the court and the parties.

11. In Chapter 7 the parental order application process is examined, with reference to the relevant rules the Family Procedure Rules 2010.

12. Chapter 8 considers alternative legal remedies where it is not possible for intended parents to apply for a parental order (or where one has been refused).

13. Finally, in Chapter 9, a number of questions are raised that should be considered by intended parents before embarking on the surrogacy process.

14. Unless stated otherwise, this book relates the legal framework in England and Wales.

CHAPTER TWO
WHAT IS SURROGACY?

1. The term surrogacy often conjures a variety of interpretations of what it might entail. Stories of celebrity couples often end up in the media and perhaps paint a glamorised image of the process. However, in reality the concept of surrogacy dates back to biblical times when Abraham and his wife Sarah, unable to conceive, enlisted the assistance of their handmaid, Hagar, to be their surrogate.

2. Surrogacy is the process whereby a woman (the surrogate) becomes pregnant with a child and following birth the child is given to another family (the intended parent(s)). The surrogate may or may not be genetically related to the child. In this jurisdiction, at birth the surrogate is always the child's legal mother and the intended parents only become legal parents until a court awards them a parental order.

3. In the joint consultation paper 'Building families though surrogacy: a new law' by the Law Commission and the Scottish Law Commission, defined surrogacy as:

   > "the practice of a woman becoming pregnant with a child that may, or may not, be genetically related to her, carrying the child, and giving birth to the child for another family (who we refer to as the "intended parents"). Under the current UK law, the surrogate is the child's legal mother at birth, and the intended parents must apply for a parental order after the birth of the child to become the legal parents of the child"[1]

---

1 'Building families though surrogacy: a new law' - https://s3-eu-west-2.amazonaws.com/lawcom-prod-storage-11jsxou24uy7q/uploads/2019/06/Surrogacy-consultation-paper.pdf

4. There has been a steady rise in the use of surrogacy as a route to parenthood, beyond what is seen in newspapers and social media. The Law Commission's wish to examine the current law (to which this book relates, as at October 2020) is illustrative of how it has come in to the 'mainstream' and viewed as a legitimate route to parenthood.

5. Lady Hale, the former President of the Supreme Court in one of her last cases described the law in relation to surrogacy as being *"fragmented and in some ways obscure"*.[2] The "fragmented" and "obscure" nature of surrogacy means that it is difficult to identify the number of children born via surrogacy each year in this jurisdiction. Equally, it is difficult to ascertain the number of children born via surrogacy in another jurisdiction to intended parents who return to live in this jurisdiction with their child.

6. The only way in which the number of people using surrogacy can be captured accurately, is by looking at the number of parental orders made each year. Parental orders, a type of Family Court order, will form a large focus of this book. They are the bespoke court order that a Family Court judge will make that recognises the intended parents as the child's parents and extinguishes the surrogate's status as a parent (and that of her husband's if she is married). Parental orders will be discussed in greater detail in Chapter 4.

7. Whilst there are profound and significant legal implications of a parental order being made, to both the intended parent(s) and the child, there is no legal obligation to acquire such an order. This makes the task identifying the total number of children born via surrogacy difficult to ascertain and the reasons why people might not apply for a parental order may vary (e.g. lack

---

2 *Whittington Hospital NHS Trust (Appellant) v XX (Respondent) [2020] UKSC 14* per Lady Hale at para [9]

of knowledge, cost or not being eligible under the current statutory criteria). However, the most recent statistics published by the Ministry of Justice in June 2020 showed that in 2012, 184 parental orders were made in England and Wales, compared to 374 and 440 in 2018 and 2019 respectively.[3] These statistics show a steady rate of increase and a willingness for courts to make those orders where the criteria are met.

8. By section 33 of the HFEA 2008, the starting point is that the woman who gives birth to the child is always the child's legal mother when the child is born. As Lady Hale observed in *Whittington Hospital NHS Trust v XX* [2020] UKSC 14, "This means that she has (in English law) parental responsibility or (in Scots law) parental responsibilities and rights. A person who has parental responsibility for a child may not surrender or transfer any part of that responsibility to another (Children Act 1989, section 2(9))."[4]

9. The consequence is that unless and until an order is made that extinguishes the surrogate's legal relationship, the child will have a lasting legal connection with the surrogate and not form part of the family of the intended parent(s). In many ways the purpose of a parental order bears striking similarities to that of an adoption order, in that it extinguishes permanently, the legal relationship between a birth parent and vests it in the adoptive parent(s) so that the child is treated as having been born to the adoptive parents. However, there is a subtle, but significant difference in that adoption orders operate in a different way in that they are bespoke Family Court orders that are intended to *replace* legal parenthood, whereas a parental order is intended to *reflect* legal parenthood.

---

3 Ministry of Justice, *Family Court Statistics Quarterly: January –March 2020 (Table 4)* available at https://www.gov.uk/government/statistics/family-court-statistics-quarterly-january-to-march-2020
4 Per Lady Hale at para [10]

10. The effect is that the parental order therefore treats the intended parent(s) as though the child was born to them from birth. Once the intended parent(s) is recognised as a legal parent, that can only be removed by the making of an adoption order or revocation of the parental order. In *G v G (parental order: revocation) [2012] EWHC 1979 (Fam)* which concerned an application by the intended father to revoke a parental order on the grounds of alleged procedural defects and concealment of the intended mother's intention to separate from the intended father. The court refused the application confirming that that there was no statutory power to set aside a parental order and that principles governing revocation should be guided by the authorities on revoking adoption orders.

The historical context of surrogacy in England and Wales

11. Prior to the 1980s there was no legal framework for surrogacy in the UK. There is therefore no quantitative data to assess how prevalent it was, other than anecdotal evidence. But from about the mid 1970s, advancements in medical science facilitated a change in how families were formed and individuals previously excluded from parenthood were able to become parents.

12. The case of *In re C (A Minor) (Wardship: Surrogacy) [1985] FLR 846,* known as the 'baby Cotton' case in the 1980s led to the Surrogacy Arrangements Act 1985. The surrogate agreed to have a child for a couple who lived abroad on a commercial basis. This was the first known case of commercial surrogacy in this jurisdiction. The case caused quite a political and moral storm and the child was made the subject of wardship proceedings in the High Court to determine where the child should live, and for some time the child was placed in foster care. Those proceedings concluded on welfare grounds that the child should be placed in the care of the intended parents and they

were given permission to remove the child from England to travel to their home country.

13. The media furore that ensued from *Re C* led to the Surrogacy Arrangements Act 1985. Under this Act, commercial surrogacy is illegal in the UK and it is a criminal offence under the same Act to advertise either for a surrogate or to be a surrogate.[5] It is also a criminal offence to negotiate a surrogacy arrangement on a commercial basis.[6] The Act remains in force today. As well as prohibiting commercial surrogacy, one of the key aspects of the Act is that surrogacy arrangements in this jurisdiction are unenforceable, i.e. where a party enters into a surrogacy arrangement and there is a dispute about where the child should live, the parties to the arrangement cannot be compelled to perform or carry out their side of the arrangement[7]. In such circumstances, where there is a dispute post birth between intended parents and a surrogate, those cases are determined on welfare, i.e. what is in the child's best interests.[8]

14. Following the birth of Louise Brown in Oldham in 1978 (the first person in the world to be born as a result of in vitro fertilisation (IVF)), The Report of the Committee of Inquiry into Human Fertilisation and Embryology (1984) (headed by Baroness Warnock, known as the 'Warnock Report') was published.

15. The concept of egg donation was introduced in 1983 which allowed for gestational surrogacy, where an embryo is created by IVF using the egg of the intended mother or donor egg and the sperm of the intended father or donor sperm which is then implanted in the surrogate. The corollary is that the surrogate is

---

5   Surrogacy Arrangements Act 1985 s3
6   Surrogacy Arrangements Act 1985 s2
7   Surrogacy Arrangements Act 1985 s1A
8   see *H (A child: Surrogacy breakdown) [2017] EWCA Civ 1798*

a "gestational carrier" but bears no genetic relationship to the child. In contrast to gestational surrogacy where the surrogate has no genetic link to the child, with traditional surrogacy, the surrogate's own eggs are used and she therefore has a genetic link to the child.

16. The Warnock Committee was unable to secure a consensus on surrogacy and the committee characterised the task they had as being one of the "most difficult problems" that they had encountered".[9] The report concluded that surrogacy arrangements, whether on altruistic or commercial grounds were "liable to moral objection".[10] The general tenor of their recommendations was the prohibition and prevention of commercial surrogacy on the basis that such arrangements were likely to enter the realms of exploitation where there were financial interests were concerned. The extent of the moral and legal ambivalence towards surrogacy at the time was perhaps best illustrated by the reluctance to allow non-profit making surrogacy services that would the subject of regulation as that would be seen to be encouraging surrogacy.

17. The Warnock Committee report eventually paved the way for the Human Fertilisation and Embryology Act 1990 ('HFEA 1990'), which provided a legal framework surrogacy in the UK on an altruistic basis – i.e. it permitted reasonable expenses to be paid to the surrogate, with commercial surrogacy remaining prohibited under the Surrogacy Arrangements Act 1985. Under the HFEA 1990 only married heterosexual couples were able to apply for parental orders, the bespoke court order required for child who is born as a result of a surrogacy arrangement to allow

---

9 Report of the Committee of Inquiry into Human Fertilisation and Embryology (1984) Cmnd 9314 para 8.17.
10 Report of the Committee of Inquiry into Human Fertilisation and Embryology (1984) Cmnd 9314 para 8.17.

the intended parent(s) to be recognised as the child's legal parent(s) in this jurisdiction.

18. The legislative framework that was shaped by the Warnock Committee adopted what in many ways is now considered to be a paternalistic approach to protect the surrogate from the risk of exploitation. However, decades later, Baroness Warnock considered that the law in relation to surrogacy was too protective of the surrogate, based on the assumption that the surrogate was most at risk of exploitation.[11]

19. Following the Warnock Report in the 1980s, The Brazier Report, chaired by legal academic Professor Margaret Brazier consider the question of surrogacy again in 1997 having been invited to consider it by the new Labour Administration. The report had three key areas upon which to address: i) whether payments, including expenses, should continue to be made to surrogates; (ii) whether a recognised body/bodies should regulate surrogacy arrangements; and ii) whether any changes were required in the Surrogacy Arrangements Act 1985 and/or (the then) Human Fertilisation and Embryology Act 1990.[12]

20. Braizer rejected calls to allow a surrogate to acquire any financial benefit from a surrogacy arrangement and preferred maintaining the principle that payments to a surrogate should be in relation to expenses arising directly from the pregnancy. Perhaps something that now seems extreme, the Brazier report recommended that the court's power to retrospectively authorise excessive payments should be removed which would render such intended parents ineligible to apply for a parental order. Overall the

---

11 See M. Warnock, "Foreword: The Need for Full Reform of the Law on Surrogacy" (2016) 4 *Journal of Medical Law and Ethics* 155, 156.

12 (1998) Cm 4068, Executive Summary para 1. Surrogacy: Review for Health Ministers of Current Arrangements for Payments and Regulation (October

Braizer Report favoured a new surrogacy legislation to consolidate their recommendations. The report was published in October 1998 but was never subsequently implemented and it is unclear whether the relevant government departments responded to the proposals.

21. The statutory framework that originated from the 1980s remained in place until reform came in the way of the HFEA 2008. Under this new act, the availability of parental orders was extended to same sex couples (in a civil partnership – or married following the Marriage (Same Sex Couples) Act 2013) or partners (whether a same sex couple or heterosexual couple) who are in an enduring family relationship. That provision came into force in April 2010. Those reforms fell short of allowing parental orders for single people.

22. However, *In the matter of Z (a child) (No 2) [2016] EWHC 1191 (Fam)*, a human rights case where a single applicant sought a declaration if incompatibly that the statutory framework that only allowed couples to apply for parental orders was a breach of his rights guaranteed by the European Convention on Human Rights (the same was also argued on behalf of the child). The High Court made the declaration sought and the government changed the law to allow single people with a genetic relationship to the child to apply to for parental orders.[13]

23. The law in relation to surrogacy is complex and has seen many changes to it over last decade. After much lobbying and many reported cases, the Law Commission for England and Wales confirmed on 4 May 2018 that the law relating to surrogacy was going to be reviewed. The Law Commission, the statutory inde-

---

13 See The Human Fertilisation and Embryology Act 2008 (Remedial) Order 2018 (SI 2018 No 1413).

pendent body created in 1965 to keep the law of England and Wales under review and to recommend reform where it is needed. The aim of the Commission is to ensure that the law is: fair, modern, simple and cost effective.

24. The Law Commission has been keen to acknowledge that the law created over 30 years ago is not fit for purpose and that the Law Commission was keen to examine to what extent the law could be updated to ensure it reflected societal change and was for purpose.

25. It is clear that there has been something of a paradigm shift in terms of societal attitudes towards surrogacy since the 1980s when laws were first passed. Recent debates in the House of Lords regarding surrogacy legislation reflect this, with law makers observing that there has been a struggle that "surrogacy policy and legislation are facing to keep pace with 21st – century attitudes and lifestyles" and that there is recognition of the "value of surrogacy as a means of helping to create new families for a range of people who might not otherwise be able to have their own children."[14]

Where do people go?

26. Notwithstanding the statutory provisions that permit altruistic surrogacy in the UK, there is often a perception amongst intended parents that undertaking surrogacy in the UK might be "risky" because of the way in which the law operates, means that the surrogate is always regarded as the legal mother unless and until a parental order is made which engenders a lack of security and uncertainty. In reality, such disputes are rare however it is compounded with the view that many intended

---

[14] Hansard, House of Lords, 14 December 2016, Vol. 777, columns 1316-1332.

parents feel there is a lack of certainty that they will be matched with a surrogate, with an immeasurable timescale.[15] Intended parents therefore often go abroad to countries where they consider that there is greater certainty around their status as parents to a child.

27. It is not however, always so straightforward. Different countries have varying standards that are applied to surrogacy practices. In countries where there is no legal framework for children who are born as a result of surrogacy arrangements, intended parents should exercise extreme caution. In the last decade there have been a number of cases that have caught the media attention that has subsequently led to surrogacy in that jurisdiction being prohibited.[16]

Conclusion

28. Whilst surrogacy is permitted in this jurisdiction, the statutory framework remains one that was largely informed by what was considered culturally and morally acceptable in the 1980s. There has been some reform in the way of the HFEA 2008, however the Law Commission's interest in the area of surrogacy law reform suggests that it is likely that there will be further changes to the law related to surrogacy at some point in the 2020s to bring the law up to date with contemporary views of society generally.

---

15 N. Gamble & H. Prosser 'Modern surrogacy practice and the need for reform' (2016) 4 *Journal of medical law and ethics* Vol 4
16 See https://www.theguardian.com/australia-news/2015/jan/20/baby-gammy-born-into-thai-surrogacy-scandal-granted-australian-citizenship

CHAPTER THREE
LEGAL PARENTHOOD AND PARENTAL RESPONSIBILITY

The basics: legal parenthood and parental responsibility

1. Before examining surrogacy in more detail, it is essential to lay the foundation of the different legal concepts that impact on surrogacy and how these concepts define the relationships of children born via surrogacy and their intended parent(s).

2. For English lawyers, the landmark House of Lords decision of *Re G (Children) (Residence: Same Sex Partner) [2006] UKHL 43* gave way to a broadened view of parenthood, acknowledging that genetic or biological parenthood was not the only form of 'natural' parenthood. In so doing, the court recognised an emerging discourse which defined 'natural' parenthood in three ways:

   a) Genetic parenthood: the provision of gametes which produce the child.
   b) Gestational parenthood: the conceiving and bearing of the child.
   c) Social and psychological parenthood: the relationship that develops through the child demanding the parent provide for their needs, initially (and at the most basic level) of feeding, nurturing, comforting and loving, and later (at the more sophisticated level) of guiding, socialising, educating and protecting.

3. Whilst English law treats parents as falling into one or more of these three sub-categories, they do not accurately describe the legal position of parenthood in English law which is contained under the concept of legal parenthood.

4. Legal parenthood in English law is a status which can only be held by two individual parents at any one time. The two individuals can be genetic, gestational or social parents, or a combination of all three (e.g. a birth mother). Legal parenthood confers an important status to the parent and child, making the child a member of the parent's family and bringing with it core responsibilities and rights. For example, entitlements on intestacy are determined by reference to legal parenthood, as are citizenship rights and the duty to maintain a child financially. Legal parenthood carries with it five important implications:

   a) the law relating to contact and where a child lives (section 10(4)(a) Children Act 1989);
   b) child maintenance (schedule 1, para.4 and 10 Children Act 1989 as amended by schedule 6 HFEA 2008);
   c) inheritance (section 48(5) HFEA 2008);
   d) "bring(ing) and defend(ing) proceedings about the child" (Baroness Hale in Re G [2006] UKHL 43 [2006] 2 FLR 629 at §32) and importantly:
   e) "mak(ing) the child a member of that person's family" [1]

5. It should be noted that whilst it is possible for legal parenthood to be terminated and changed, it can only happen in a limited amount of circumstances (i.e. surrogacy and adoption) as shall be explored in this book in the context of surrogacy. It is important to note that legal parenthood differs from the legal concept of parental responsibility.

6. As Theis J observed in *Re B (Adoption: Surrogacy and Parental Responsibility) [2018] EWFC 86*

   "Parental responsibility does not define parenthood, a legal parent may or may not have parental responsibility, equally a person can have parental responsibility without being recog-

---

1 *AB v CD [2013] EWHC 1418 (Fam)* at para 2

nised as a parent (for example, under a child arrangements order or special guardianship order in their favour)."²

7. In legal terms, the status of who is and is not a legal parent is afforded great importance. The former President of the Family Division, Sir James Munby observed that:

> "The question of who, in law, is or are the parent(s) of a child born as a result of treatment carried out under this legislation – the issue which confronts me here – is dealt with in Part 2, sections 33-47, of the 2008 Act. It is, as a moment's reflection will make obvious, a question of the most fundamental gravity and importance. What, after all, to any child, to any parent, never mind to future generations and indeed to society at large, can be more important, emotionally, psychologically, socially and legally, than the answer to the question: **Who is my parent? Is this my child?**" (emphasis added)³

8. Whilst this is a quote from a judgment that did not relate to surrogacy, it related to the operation of statutory provisions under the HFEA 2008 and parental status, and so is relevant in the context of surrogacy where it is necessary to establish who is a child's legal parent.

9. Parental responsibility is a legal concept defined by statute and it is a concept that that is also afforded great importance by parents, lawyers, judges and all professionals involved in the lives of children. The Children Act 1989 defines parental responsibility as 'all rights, duties, powers, responsibilities and authority which by law a parent of a child has in relation to the child and his property'⁴. There is no attempt made by the

---

2 Per Theis J at para [59]
3 *Re A and others (Human Fertilisation and Embryology) (Legal Parenthood: written consent)* [2015] EWHC 2602 at para [3]
4 Children Act 1989 s3(1)

Children Act 1989 to list endlessly matters that may fall under the scope of parental responsibility. But it is a concept that is central to other aspects concerning the welfare of children, and will arise in applications concerning, for example, when one holder of parental responsibility wishes to stop or prohibit another holder of parental responsibility from taking particular step in relation to a child (e.g. a prohibited steps order to prevent a child being removed from the jurisdiction); or where one holder of parental responsibility wishes to determine a specific issue which may arise in connection to parental responsibility (e.g. a specific issue order to order that a medical procedure take place). Important decisions in respect of a child's life will therefore require agreement by all those who hold parental responsibility in respect of a child, e.g.:

- Medical treatment;

- Religious upbringing;

- Where a child should live;

- Where a child is educated;

- Significant movement of the child (i.e. to leave the country for on a temporary basis (e.g. a holiday) or on a permanent basis);

10. Unlike legal parenthood where no more than two individuals may hold such status, with parental responsibility, more than two people may share it in respect of a child at the same time. It should be noted that simply because more than two people share parental responsibility it does not operate in a way that allows a block to veto the other (e.g. if three people hold parental responsibility and two of those people agree in relation to a particular aspect of parental responsibility, it does not trump the third person).

Acquisition of parental responsibility

11. There are a number of ways in which an individual may acquire parental responsibility.

Married and unmarried couples

12. In circumstances where a child's mother and father were married to each other at the time of a child's birth, each of the parents automatically acquires parental responsibility (Children Act 1989, S2(1)). Where the child's parents are *not* married at the time of the child's birth, the birth mother automatically acquires parental responsibility (Children Act 1989, S2(2)a) and the father will subsequently acquire parental responsibility if: i) he is registered as the child's father on the child's birth certificate; ii) he enters into a parental responsibility agreement with the mother; or iii) a court so orders. The Adoption and Children Act 2002, which amended the Children Act 1989, enabled unmarried fathers to acquire parental responsibility if registered as the child's father (Children Act 1989, S4(1)(a)). That provision came into force on 1 December 2003, however it does not operate retrospectively (i.e. fathers who did not acquire parental responsibility at birth *pre-December 2003* but were named on the child's birth certificate do not subsequently acquire parental responsibility.

Child arrangements order

13. A child arrangements order is an order made by a Family Court that identifies where and with whom a child shall live and how often a child shall spend time with the other person.[5] However, the orders are not exclusive to parents and may be made in favour of other adults in respect of a child, such as grandparents, aunts and uncles providing they meet the relevant criteria to

---

5   Prior to 2014, they were known as "residence and contact orders".

apply for the order or a court has given them permission to apply. Child arrangement orders are an important order in respect of parental responsibility, as with it, they can attach an ability for the holder of the child arrangements order to acquire parental responsibility.

14. By s12(2) of the Children Act 1989, when the court makes a child arrangement order and the person who is not a parent or guardian of the child concerned and the order specifies that the child shall live with that person, then that person shall have parental responsibility in respect of that child for the duration of the order. Similarly, by S12(2A)(b) of the Children Act 1989, where the court makes a child arrangements order to regulate how much time a child should spend with an adult, the court may also provide in the order that that person is to have parental responsibility.

Acquisition of parental responsibility by virtue of the Human Fertilisation and Embryology 2008

15. Section 2 of the Children Act 1989 was amended in 2009 to create a statutory provision for parental responsibility where a child has a parent by virtue of s42 or s43 of the HFEA 2008.

    Where a child:

    a) Has a parent by virtue of s 42 (i.e. treatment provided to a woman who is a party to a civil partnership or marriage at the time of treatment); or
    b) Has a parent by virtue of s43 (treatment provided to a woman who agrees to a second woman being parent) and is a person to whom the Family Law Reform Act 1987, applies, the mother and the other parent shall each have parental responsibility for the child.

16. Where a child has a parent by virtue of s43, but is not within the Family Law Reform Act 1989, s 1(3), the child's mother shall have parental responsibility for the child and the other parent shall have parental responsibility for the child if she acquires it in accordance with the Act. [6]

17. These provisions only apply in circumstances where the child is carried by a woman as a result of treatment received on or after 1 September 2009.

18. By s4ZA of the Children Act 1989 where a child has a parent by virtue of section 43 of the HFEA 2008 and is not a person to whom section 1(3) of the Family Law Reform Act 1987 applies, that parent shall acquire parental responsibility for the child if— (a) she becomes registered as a parent of the child under any of the enactments specified in s4ZA(2); (b) she and the child's mother make an agreement providing for her to have parental responsibility for the child; or (c) the court, on her application, orders that she shall have parental responsibility for the child.

Termination of parental responsibility

19. Where parental responsibility has been acquired as a result of a child arrangements order under s12 of the Children Act 1989, parental responsibility shall last until the child reaches 18 or until the order is discharged by the court.

20. Once a parental order is made, conferring legal parenthood on the intended parent, they will also have parental responsibility (if they did not already have it by the making of a child arrangements order). Similarly, parental responsibility may only be removed from a parent by court order (see *Re D (A Child) [2014] EWCA Civ 315*) or on the cessation of a child arrange-

---

[6] The circumstances in which a parent may acquire parental responsibility are outlined in s4ZA of the Children Act 1989.

ments order that conferred parental responsibility and there is no other order in place (e.g. a parental order or an adoption order).

Relevance to surrogacy

21. Both legal parenthood and parental responsibility are relevant when considering surrogacy. Where a child is born as a result of a surrogacy arrangement, legal parenthood and parental responsibility are not automatically acquired. It is also worth noting that this is regardless of where a child is born.

22. In many countries (such as states like California in the United States of America), intended parents will acquire full parental rights either prior to birth, *in utero* (usually by way of a 'pre-birth order') or immediately post the birth of the child that extinguishes the surrogate's parental status (and that of her husband if married) permanently and transfers it to the intended parent(s). However, unlike cases of international adoption where in a limited number of cases where specific criteria are met, a court order from another country which recognises the intended parents as parents in that jurisdiction can be recognised here, there is currently no such provision for surrogacy in this country. This could therefore have consequences for intended parents when they arrive in this country if they do not regularise their legal relationship with their child as soon as possible. If for example, a child required medical treatment, they would require the child's legal parents to give consent to such treatment, which can only be valid if it is given by the holder(s) of parental responsibility, so it becomes ever more important that intended parents take steps to secure their legal status with children born via surrogacy, whether they arise from domestic or international arrangements. Speaking extra-judicially, Mrs. Justice Theis DBE, one of the main High Court

Judges who deals with applications for parental orders in international cases, observed that her concern *"is about people who are not making [parental order] applications"* and that *"There's a ticking legal timebomb that might arise later on through [the parents'] deaths, testamentary [inheritance] issues and through parents splitting up – or even simply if passports need to be renewed."*[7]

23. The bigger problem is those who do not apply, with many intended parents resenting have to legally justify (possibly again if it was an international arrangement) that their child is theirs. In addition to this, the process of applying for a parental order might be considered by some as complex and are therefore put off applying.[8]

Conclusion

24. Legal parenthood and parental responsibility are key legal concepts which should be respected and appreciated by anyone embarking on the surrogacy process. There is a profound interplay in terms of both concepts and how they are acquired in surrogacy arrangements. It is also important to ensure that the difference between legal parenthood and parental responsibility are acknowledged given the significant differences in respect of the power they afford to an individual.

---

7   https://www.theguardian.com/lifeandstyle/2015/may/18/unregistered-surrogate-born-children-creating-legal-timebomb-judge-warns available on 2 May 2020
8   N. Gamble & H. Prosser 'Modern surrogacy practice and the need for reform' (2016) 4 *Journal of medical law and ethics* Vol 4

CHAPTER FOUR
PARENTAL ORDERS AND THE PARENTAL ORDER CRITERIA

1. As discussed in the preceding chapters, under English law the woman who gives birth to the child is always regarded as the child's mother (even if she is a gestational surrogate). Regardless of legal orders or judgments obtained in the jurisdiction of birth, the birth mother is always seen as the legal mother under English law. If the surrogate is married, then he is the legal father. It is quite possible therefore, to have a surrogacy arrangement in which the gametes of the intended mother and father are used to create the embryo and if the surrogate is married, at birth neither intended parent will have any status in relation to the child, despite the child being biologically related to both intended parents.

2. The most appropriate way for intended parents to acquire legal status is by obtaining a parental order. It is the bespoke order that must be sought for children born through surrogacy to confer parental rights on the intended parents and extinguish the surrogate's parental rights. In Chapter 8 alternative orders are discussed where it is not possible for a parental order to be made.

3. The parental order is similar to an adoption order in that it extinguishes the surrogate's (and husband if applicable) parental status and transfers it exclusively to the intended parent(s). The status conferred by a parental order is that the child is treated in law as a child of the applicants (section 54(1) of the HFEA 2008).

4. However, whilst there are similar in the nature, adoption orders and parental orders are both bespoke orders in their own right. An adoption order is significant in that it is designed to replace a child's legal parentage in favour of the adoptive parent. With a parental order it is also significant, but is transferring legal parentage to the intended parents who, from conception, were always intended to be the child's legal parent. Both orders bring with them important distinctions that will be important in terms of a child's life story.

5. The judges who hear these cases have regarded them as "transformative" orders because of the legal significance that they bring with them for the child and the intended parent. Section 54 of the Human Fertilisation and Embryology Act 2008 deals with the criteria that must be met in order for a parental order to be made.

6. In the case of *Re X (a child) (Surrogacy: time limit) [2014] EWHC 3135 (Fam)*, a case that will be discussed at greater length later in this chapter, Sir James Munby P characterised the s54 criteria as follows:

> *"Section 54 goes to the most fundamental aspects of status and, transcending even status, to the very identity of the child as a human being: who he is and who his parents are. It is central to his being, whether as an individual or as a member of his family. As Ms Isaacs correctly puts it, this case is fundamentally about Xs identity and his relationship with the commissioning parents. Fundamental as these matters must be to commissioning parents they are, if anything, even more fundamental to the child. A parental order has, to adopt Theis J's powerful expression, a transformative effect, not just in its effect on the child's legal relationships with the surrogate and commissioning parents but also, to adopt the guardian's words in the present case, in relation to the practical and psychological real-*

ities of X's identity. A parental order, like an adoption order, has an effect extending far beyond the merely legal. It has the most profound personal, emotional, psychological, social and, it may be in some cases, cultural and religious, consequences. It creates what Thorpe LJ in Re J (Adoption: Non-Patrial) [1998] INLR 424, 429, referred to as "the psychological relationship of parent and child with all its far-reaching manifestations and consequences." Moreover, these consequences are lifelong and, for all practical purposes, irreversible: see G v G (Parental Order: Revocation) [2012] EWHC 1979 (Fam), [2013] 1 FLR 286, to which I have already referred. And the court considering an application for a parental order is required to treat the child's welfare throughout his life as paramount: see in In re L (A Child) (Parental Order: Foreign Surrogacy) [2010] EWHC 3146 (Fam), [2011] Fam 106, [2011] 1 FLR 1143. X was born in December 2011, so his expectation of life must extend well beyond the next 75 years. Parliament has therefore required the judge considering an application for a parental order to look into a distant future."[1]

7. Similarly, in *Re A and B (Children) (Surrogacy: Parental Orders: Time Limits) [2015] EWHC 911 (Fam)* Russell J observed:

   "Parental orders create a permanent parent-child relationship throughout the children's lifetimes which reflect the reality of their particular situation about which they are both already aware. Thus parental orders are explicitly the most apposite orders to be made in keeping with the children's welfare throughout their lives, and which confer important status and rights over and above parental responsibility."[2]

---

1   Per Sir James Munby P at para [54]
2   Per Russell J at para [59]

8. Without being made the subject of a parental order, children born via surrogacy are potentially left in a state of legal limbo. For example, complex legal matters such as inheritance or citizenship rights might not be conferred if a child is not the subject of a parental order. The implications are stark and may result in intended parents assuming erroneously that the child will automatically be entitled to benefit from an estate on death or acquire a particular nationality automatically.

9. The criteria for making a parental order are set out in section 54 and section 54A of the HFEA 2008. Section 54 relates to applications made by two people and section 54A relates to applications made by single people.

10. The criteria for two applicants is as follows:

    - The child has been carried by a woman who is not one of the applicants, as a result of the placing in her of an embryo or sperm and eggs or her artificial insemination – s54(1)(a);

    - The gametes of at least one of the applicants were used to bring about the creation of the embryo – s54(1)(b);

    - Applicants must be married, in a civil partnership or two persons living as partners "enduring family relationship" – s54(2)(a-c);

    - Application must be made within 6 months of the child's birth – s54(3);

    - At the time of the application and the making of the order, the child's home must be with the applicants – (s54(4)(a);

    - At the time of the application and the making of the order, either or both of the applicants must be domiciled in the

UK or in the Channel Islands or the Isle of Man – s54(4)(b);

- The applicants must be over 18 at the time of the making of the order – s54(5);

- The court must be satisfied that the surrogate (and her husband if applicable) freely, and with full understanding of what is involved, have agreed unconditionally to the making of an order – s54(6);

- The court must be satisfied that no money or other benefit (other than for expenses reasonably incurred) has been given or received by either of the applicants for or in consideration of (a) the making of the order, (b) any agreement required by subsection (6), (c) the handing over of the child to the applicants, or (d) the making of arrangements with a view to the making of the order – s54(8).

11. The criteria for a single applicant prescribed by s54A is identical to the criteria under s54 for two applicants save for the requirement that the gametes of the single applicant **must** be used to bring about the embryo under s54A(1)(b). This means therefore that an embryo created using double gamete donation (whether for a single or joint application) would not qualify for a parental order as the gametes of the applicant or one of the applicants must be used.

12. The rest of this chapter shall focus on some of the issues that have arisen in meeting the criteria outlined above.

The child has been carried by a woman who is not one of the applicants, as a result of the placing in her of an embryo or sperm and eggs or her artificial insemination – s54(1)(a);

13. The key issue to which this provision relates is perhaps the essential characteristic that makes it a surrogacy arrangement. The child must have been carried by a woman who is not one of the applicants as a result of some form of embryo transfer (in the case of gestational surrogacy) or sperm or eggs via artificial insemination. Thus, an arrangement whereby a man has sexual intercourse with another woman who becomes pregnant and then wishes to apply for a parental order with his spouse/partner would not be eligible for a parental order.

The gametes of at least one of the applicants were used to bring about the creation of the embryo – s54(1)(b) (and s54A(1)(b) in respect of a single applicant)

14. There has been much debate amongst legal scholars as to whether parental orders should be available in cases where double gamete donation has taken place in the case of a couple, or single applicant. As the law stands currently, it is not possible for such individuals to qualify for a parental order. Much of the debate around the necessity to have the gametes of one of the applicants is that, to remove that requirement enters the realm of what many consider to be "baby buying" or "buying designer babies". The difficulty with the provision is that whilst would-be intended parents are prohibited from applying for a parental order in such cases, that does not stop it happening abroad in jurisdictions such as some states in the United States of America (e.g. California) and some provinces of Canada (e.g. Ontario and British Columbia) and some states in Australia (e.g. Victoria). In such cases, the applicant or applicants, will be unable to apply for a parental order in this jurisdiction and will have to

find some other legal means by which they can be recognised as parents, which is discussed further in Chapter 8.

15. The Law Commission is currently exploring (October 2020) whether the law should be amended to allow parental orders in cases where there is no biological connection as a result of a "medical necessity". It is not clear how "medical necessity" would be defined by law. Plainly it is intended to address issues where the intended parent(s) have fertility issues or for other medical reasons, however under the current proposals it is only proposed that such a change apply to surrogacy arrangements undertaken in the UK.

Applicants must be married, in a civil partnership or two persons living as partners "enduring family relationship" – s54(2)(a-c);

16. Plainly, this criterion only applies to applications made by two people. In respect of marriage or a civil partnership, there is no requirement for the duration of either form of union. However, the statute does not define what amounts to an "enduring family relationship".

17. The question of what amounted to an enduring family relationship was considered by Hedley J in the context of an adoption case in *T & M v Occ & C [2020] EWHC 964* where the court observed:

> "Clearly the crucial words are "living as partners in an enduring family relationship." These words are no doubt chosen so as not to require the residence of both in the same property. That is not surprising as historically many a parent has had to work abroad whilst the family remained at home without in anyway imperilling an enduring family relationship. Nor is that unusual today with people having to move jobs often at short notice. What is required is: first, an

unambiguous intention to create and maintain family life, and secondly, a factual matrix consistent with that intention. That is clearly a question of fact and degree in each case"[3]

18. The same question of what amounts to an enduring family relationship was subsequently considered by Russell J in Re *F & M (Children) (Thai Surrogacy) (Enduring family relationship) [2016] EWHC 1594 (Fam)*[4], the application for parental orders concerned twins born in Thailand as a result of a commercial surrogacy agreement entered into by the applicants and a gestational surrogate.

19. In that case the applicants' relationship commenced in April 2014. The twins were born in Thailand in January 2015 using a donor egg and the sperm of the first applicant.

20. The applicants made applications for parental orders on time and the court directed, in the usual way, that they provide statements and the parental order reporter provide a report (the role of the parental order reporter is discussed in Chapter 6). In respect of the question of whether the applicants' relationship could be considered to be an enduring family relationship, Russell J observed.

> *"16. The HFEA does not define what an "enduring relationship" is and it was submitted on their behalf that the Court would wish to consider the nature of the applicants' relationship having regard to the specific facts of this case as set out in their joint statement and in the POR's assessment of the couple; that is the approach which I intend to take. It mirrors the approach taken in previous cases where parental orders have been made (of which more below) and the nature and*

---

3 per Hedley J at para [16]
4 See also *Re A (A Child : Surrogacy: S.54 Criteria) [2020] EWHC 1426 (Fam)*

structure of any family relationship must be one which is in, the greatest part, based on the facts of each specific case and family. The families in which children live and are brought up are increasingly diverse and often more fluid than in the past; the enactment of the HFEA 2008 came about in recognition of this change. I have been referred to the Parliamentary debates which took place at the time.

17. Counsel for the applicants made reference to the notes to the Family Court Practice 2015 (at page 374) which set out, in relation to the definition under the Adoption and Children Act 2002 (ACA 2002), that 'To establish that a couple are 'living as partners in an enduring family relationship', there must first be an unambiguous intention to create and maintain family life and, second, a factual matrix consistent with that intention. Both matters are a question of fact and degree in each case. There is no requirement that both partners should reside in the same property (*Re T&M Adoption [2010] EWHC 964 (Fam)*, [2011] 1 FLR 1487).'

18. Sir James Munby, President, considered the definition of "couple" pursuant to section 54(1) in *Re Z [2015] EWFC 73*; in his judgment he said (at [13]) that the HFEA 2008 had brought the definition of "couple" in line with the definition of "couple" in *section 144(4) of the Adoption and Children Act (ACA) 2002*; he said that since the Marriage (Same Sex Couples) Act 2013 came into force on 13th March 2014 the definition in both Acts now extends to married couples of the same sex. The ACA 2002 defined 'couple' at s. 144(4) as follows; 'In this Act, a couple means; (a) a married couple, or (b) two people (whether of different sexes or the same sex) living as partners in an enduring family relationship.'"[5]

---

5   Per Russell J at para 16-18

21. The court acknowledged that there was limited reported case law concerning the definition of "enduring family relationship". It was submitted on behalf of the applicants that it was not necessary for the court to "read down" the statute (pursuant to s.3(1) of the Human Rights Act 1998) and that a straightforward reading of the statue applied to the relevant facts of the case would entitle the court to conclude that the applicants were in an enduring family relationship. The court examined the parliamentary debates using Hansard and concluded that Parliament's intention had been for the court to decide what amounted to an enduring family relationship. The court noted that in the present case the applicants' relationship had started (significantly, it seems) prior to the commencement of IVF treatment. When the children were born in January 2015 the applicants had been in a relationship for ten months and by the time they made the applications to the court for parental orders they had been together as a couple for fourteen months and living together for a year. By the time of the final hearing they had been in a relationship for almost two years.

22. Having satisfied herself that Parliament had intended the court to determine what an enduring family relationship was, Russell J concluded that the facts in this case indicated that the applicants were in an enduring family relationship. The court considered the remaining s54 factors and made a parental order.

23. In *Re N (Surrogacy: Enduring Family Relationship: Child's Home) [2019] EWFC 21* Theis J was concerned with an application for a parental order in relation to a child born as a result of a surrogacy agreement where the applicants (who were not married or in a civil partnership) had separated at the time of the hearing. The case concerned the court's interpretation of s54(2) of the HFEA 2008.

24. The applicant (K) and first respondent (L) applied for the parental order with respect to their 16-month-old daughter who had been born following a gestational surrogacy arrangement in Canada in 2017 from a donor egg and K's gametes.

25. They applied for a parental order in March 2018. Their relationship fell into difficulties and L left the family home. In August 2018 the court made a child arrangement order in their favour and granted them both parental responsibility. Whilst child arrangements were eventually agreed between the parties, it was not clear whether a parental order could be made as s54(2) HFEA 2008 required the applicants to be living as partners in an enduring family relationship, and s54(4) HFEA 2008 required the child to have a home with the applicants.

26. In respect of s54(2) HFEA 2008, the court opined the requirement that they be living as partners in an enduring family relationship that *"s 54 (2) is silent as to the need for the requirement to be linked to any particular time. In those circumstances the court should be alert not to read in any requirement that is not there in the primary legislation."* [6]. The court considered Article 8 of the European Convention on Human Rights. As the child had lived with K and L all her life and was biologically related to K the effect of not making an order would interfere with their right to family life. It was necessary therefore to consider the provisions of s54(2) purposively, so that the requirement for an enduring family relationship was not to be linked to any particular time.

27. More recently, Keehan J applied a similar approach in *Re A (Surrogacy: s.54 Criteria) [2020] EWHC 1426 (Fam)* in circumstances where the intended parents entered into a domestic surrogacy arrangement using both of their gametes. The intended parents, who were not married, separated prior during

---

6 Per Theis J at para [34]

the pregnancy of the child. Post birth the intended father had limited involvement with the child and it was only after the child was almost 3 years old that the intended father indicated his wish to be part of the child's life. The case deals with the interpretation of a number of the s54 criteria as the application was also made after the 6-month time limit and the intended parents were not living together at the time of the application and when the order was made (the latter issue is discussed further below). In respect of the enduring family relationship requirement Keehan J identified a number of factors that enabled the court to find that the intended parents had been in an enduring family relationship:

i. Prior to the surrogacy arrangement the intended parents were in an enduring relationship;
ii. They wished to have a family and desperately wanted a child of their own;
iii. They agreed to pursue a surrogacy arrangement and each provided their gametes to produce embryos for transplantation into the surrogate
iv. At the time of the joint application for a parental order in December 2019 both of the intended parents were committed to playing key roles in the child's life and were committed to his care and well-being;
v. At the time of the application both of the intended parents had and/ or wished to have a close relationship with the child;
vi. Both of the intended parents were committed to working together to promote the welfare best interests of the child throughout his childhood and beyond;
vii. The intended parents wished to have their biological status as the child's parents recognised in law.[7]

---

7   see para [55]

28. This case highlights that courts hearing applications for parental orders are prepared to take as broad an interpretation as possible to establish that an enduring family relationship exists. Each case is therefore fact specific where an issue of interpretation arises and it will be a fact-finding exercise by the trial judge to determine whether an enduring family relationship can be said to be established in that particular case.

Application must be made within 6 months of the child's birth – s54(3)

29. The criteria that an application for a parental order must be made within 6 months of the birth of the child until 2014 was viewed as a fixed and final date, albeit arbitrary in nature. Thus, in cases where the application was said to be made "out of time" the application could not progress further and the intended parents would have to pursue a different form of legal order to regularise their legal relationship with the child.

30. In *JP v LP & Others [2014] EWHC 595 (Fam)*, King J (as she then was), was concerned with a domestic surrogacy arrangement where the intended parents had subsequently separated but prior to separation had not sought a parental order. The case came before King J and an application for a parental order was made when the child was 7 ½ months old - i.e. 6 weeks beyond the statutory limit. The application for a parental order was dismissed. King J observed that:

> *"..s54(3) says that the parties **must** apply for the order during the period of 6 months beginning with the day on which the child is born. There is no provision within the Act to provide for a discretionary extension to the statutory time limit and no one sought to argue that the court could, or should, whether by means of the use of its inherent jurisdiction or oth-*

> *erwise, seek to circumnavigate the mandatory provisions of the statute."*[8] (emphasis in original)

31. The outcome in that case was that the child was to remain a ward of court until further other, a shared residence order[9] in favour of the intended parents, all matters of parental responsibility were to be delegated to the intended parents jointly and the surrogate was prohibited from exercising her parental responsibility without permission of the court.

32. As a side note, *JP v LP* also highlighted other aspects of the statutory framework, namely section 2 of the Surrogacy Arrangements Act 1985 which prohibits negotiating surrogacy arrangements for a commercial basis. The parties had instructed solicitors to prepare a surrogacy agreement which, as King J observed whilst preparing such agreements can be undertaken lawfully free of charge, the solicitors were committing a criminal offence in contravention of section 2 of the 1985 Act.

33. However, notwithstanding the 6-month time limit, that provision came under greater scrutiny in *Re X (A Child) (Surrogacy: Time Limit) [2014] EWHC 3135 (Fam)*.

34. The application in *Re X* was made over 2 years after the child's birth - thus it was over 18 months out of time. The question was whether the court could "read down" – i.e. to interpret the statute applying Human Rights principles under the ECHR to arrive at a sensible conclusion.

35. Sir James Munby P said this:

> *"Where in the light of all this does the six-month period specified in section 54(3) stand? Can Parliament really have*

---

8   Per King J at para [29]
9   i.e. what would now be known as a 'shared lives with' child arrangements order

intended that the gate should be barred forever if the application for a parental order is lodged even one day late? I cannot think so. Parliament has not explained its thinking, but given the transcendental importance of a parental order, with its consequences stretching many, many decades into the future, can it sensibly be thought that Parliament intended the difference between six months and six months and one day to be determinative and one day's delay to be fatal? I assume that Parliament intended a sensible result. Given the subject matter, given the consequences for the commissioning parents, never mind those for the child, to construe section 54(3) as barring forever an application made just one day late is not, in my judgment, sensible. It is the very antithesis of sensible; it is almost nonsensical."[10]

36. In considering whether it was open to the court in *Re X* to make a parental order where the application was made outside the stipulated time period, Munby P sought guidance from the observations of Lord Penzance in *Howard v Boddington* (1872) 2 PD 203. Lord Penzance observed:

"The real question in all these cases is this: A thing has been ordered by the legislature to be done. What is the consequence if it is not done? In the case of statutes that are said to be imperative, the Courts have decided that if it is not done the whole thing fails, and the proceedings that follow upon it are all void. On the other hand, when the Courts hold a provision to be mandatory or directory, they say that, although such provision may not have been complied with, the subsequent proceedings do not fail. Still, whatever the language, the idea is a perfectly distinct one. There may be many provisions in Acts of Parliament which, although they are not strictly obeyed, yet do not appear to the Court to be of that material importance to the subject-matter to which they refer, as that the legislature

---

10 Per Sir James Munby P at para [55]

could have intended that the non-observance of them should be followed by a total failure of the whole proceedings. On the other hand, there are some provisions in respect of which the Court would take an opposite view, and would feel that they are matters which must be strictly obeyed, otherwise the whole proceedings that subsequently follow must come to an end. Now the question is, to which category does the provision in question in this case belong?

... I believe, as far as any rule is concerned, you cannot safely go further than that in each case you must look to the subject-matter; consider the importance of the provision that has been disregarded, and the relation of that provision to the general object intended to be secured by the Act; and upon a review of the case in that aspect decide whether the matter is what is called imperative or only directory."[11]

37. Toulson LJ, as he then was, observed in *Dharmaraj v Hounslow London Borough Council [2011] EWCA Civ 312* that:

"*The modern approach towards breach of a statutory procedural requirement is to consider the underlying purpose of the requirement and whether it follows from consideration of that legislative purpose that any departure from the precise letter of the statute, however minor, should amount to the document being regarded as a nullity."*[12]

38. Munby P sought to rely on two further authorities to deal with the issues as to the court's role in respect of statutory interpretation. In *Newbold and others v Coal Authority [2013] EWCA Civ 584* Sir Stanley Burnton observed:

---

11 Per Lord Penzance in *Howard v Boddington* (1872) 2 PD 203 at pages 210-211
12 Per Toulson LJ in *Dharmaraj v Hounslow London Borough Council* [2011] EWCA Civ 312, [2011] PTSR 1523 at para 25

"In all cases, one must first construe the statutory ... requirement in question. It may require strict compliance with a requirement as a condition of its validity ... Against that, on its true construction a statutory requirement may be satisfied by what is referred to as adequate compliance. Finally, it may be that even non-compliance with a requirement is not fatal. In all such cases, it is necessary to consider the words of the statute ... , in the light of its subject matter, the background, the purpose of the requirement, if that is known or determined, and the actual or possible effect of non-compliance on the parties. We assume that Parliament in the case of legislation ... would have intended a sensible ... result." [13]

39. Relying on *Khakh v Independent Safeguarding Authority* [2013] EWCA Civ 1341, Munby P opined:

"[Khakh] *was a case where the relevant provisions of the Safeguarding Vulnerable Groups Act 2006 provided that the judge in the Crown Court "must inform the person at the time he is convicted" that his name would be included on the statutory barring lists. The judge failed to do so. Explaining why Parliament cannot fairly have intended that the consequence of the judge's failure should be that the appellant's inclusion on these lists was a nullity, Elias LJ gave as one of his reasons (para 10) that:*

"the scheme is designed to protect children and vulnerable adults, and I cannot believe that Parliament can have intended that a failure by the judge should undermine that vital public objective." [14]

---

13 Per Sir Stanley Burnton in *Newbold and other v Coal Authority* [2013] EWCA Civ 584, [2014] 1 WLR 1288 at para 70
14 Per Munby P at para [65]

40. Whilst each case will always be fact specific, where a court is invited to "read down" the s54 criteria, the *ratio* in *Re X* can be distilled into the following principles to which the court must have regard:

The Re X Checklist:

 i. The statutory subject matter;
 ii. The background;
 iii. The purpose of the requirement (if known);
 iv. Its importance;
 v. Its relation to the general object intended to be secured by the Act;
 vi. The actual or possible impact of non-compliance on the parties;
 vii. Can Parliament have fairly been taken to have intended total invalidity?
 viii. Is any departure from the precise letter of the statue, however minor, fatal?

41. Once the court has undertaken that analysis, the final principle to which the court must have regard is the assumption that Parliament intended a sensible result.

Assessing the impact of Re X

42. The judgment in *Re X* marked a significant landmark in the statutory framework under s54, paving the way for other challenges in respect of what was at first considered to be a strictly rigid criteria.

Single applicants

43. Many legal commentators argued that the reform of the Human Fertilisation and Embryology Act 1990 that was created by the

2008 Act was a missed opportunity to extend the reforms further to permit applications for parental orders for single individuals. Many compared this to the ability of single parents to adopt or single women to undergo IVF treatment, and therefore seemed inherently discriminatory that single applicants in surrogacy cases were not afforded the same right.

44. In any event, in *Re Z (A child: Human Fertilisation and Embryology Act: Parental Order) [2015] EWFC 73* the applicant father invited the court to grant such an application, adopting a similar approach to *Re X* – i.e. to interpret the statute in a way that ensures that it is compliant with the ECHR and extend the provision of parental orders to single applicants.

45. The intended father had lawfully entered into a gestational surrogacy agreement in the USA and obtained all relevant orders in that jurisdiction conferring parental rights to the father.

46. The father applied for a parental order upon his return to the UK. But for one matter (i.e. the issue of a single parent applying for a parental order), the application was unproblematic – he met the rest of the criteria with little difficulty. The application for a parental order was supported by the child's guardian.

47. The case was heard before Munby P who refused to grant the application for a parental order. However, the question of whether the applicant should seek declaratory relief by way of a declaration of incompatibility was left open which led to an application of a declaration of incompatibility in *Z (A Child) (No 2) [2016] EWHC 1191*.

48. When the Human Rights Act 1998 came into force in October 2000, it established that human rights contained in the ECHR form part of our domestic law by ensuring that:

i. All UK law must be interpreted, so far as it is possible, in a way that is compatible with the ECHR;

ii. Where an Act of Parliament breaches these rights, the courts can declare the legislation to be incompatible with those rights. This does not affect the validity of the law – this does not transgress the doctrine of parliamentary sovereignty, as it remains a matter for Parliament to decide whether or not to amend the law;

iii. It is unlawful for any public authority to act incompatibly with human rights (unless under a statutory duty to act in that way), and anyone whose rights have been violated can bring court proceedings against the public authority.

49. The intended father therefore sought a declaration that s54(1) of the HFEA 2008 was incompatible with the rights of the father and the child (Article 8 – right to respect to private and family life and Article 14 – protection from discrimination). The application for a declaration of incompatibility was supported by the child's guardian.

50. The Government conceded to a declaration of incompatibility, however despite the case concluding in May 2016, it was only at the end of 2017 that the Government drafted a remedial order that would change the law that would allow single intended parents to apply for parental orders.

51. The remedial order, which eventually came into force in January 2019 introduced section 54A to the 2008 Act, which allows for parental orders to be made in favour of one person. This allows single parents of children born through surrogacy to apply for a parental order where their gametes have been used. It will have great ramifications for single parents who wish to secure their

parenthood and recognise the biological link between themselves and their child (which an adoption order would not do).

52. As described above, it is important to note that the new amendment only applies to single intended parents where their gametes were used. So, in cases of double gamete donation a parental order is not available. Where the criteria for a parental order is not met, this is discussed in Chapter 8.

At the time of the application and the making of the order, the child's home must be with the applicants -(s54(4)(a);

53. Following the approach taken by the courts in Re X, it has enabled the courts to take a similar approach to other aspects of the s54 criteria. By s54(4)(a) of the HFEA 2008, at the time when the application is made and when the order is made, the child's home must be with the applicant. It is easy to see how issues satisfying this criteria may arise in the context of family relationships, e.g. what happens if a couple separate after the application is made and are living in separate homes by the time the order is due to be made? Is that a bar to a parental order being made? Recent cases suggest that it is not an automatic bar, but each case will, as one might expect, turn on their own facts.

The "reading down" principles

54. In *Re X* the intended parents were separated at the time the application was issued, however they remained married within the meaning of section 54(2)(a). However, by the time the matter came before Munby P, the intended parents had reconciled. In *Re X*, the court observed that "*The real question arises in relation to section 54(4)(a): Can it be said that X's "home" was "with" them at the time of the application..*"[15]

---

15 See Munby P in Re X (A Child) (Surrogacy: Time limit) [2014] EWHC 3135 (Fam) at para 66

55. Speaking extra-judicially in 2014, the then President of the Supreme Court, Lord Neuberger of Abbotsbury, observed:

> *"...parliament has given the judges of the UK a new and significant power, in that we <u>are positively enjoined to construe statutes in such a way as to enable them to comply with the Convention</u>, a provision which is equivalent to section 32(1) of the Charter. This section 3 power has been interpreted by the UK Supreme Court as permitting courts to interpret statutes in a way which some may say amounts not so much to construction as to demolition and reconstruction. <u>In other words, we can give provisions meanings which they could not possibly bear if the normal rules of statutory interpretation applied.</u>"* [16](emphasis added)

56. The House of Lords embraced such an approach a decade earlier in *Ghaidan v Godin-Mendoza [2004] 2 AC 557*. Lord Nicholls of Birkenhead opined:

> *"From this the conclusion which seems inescapable is that the mere fact the language under consideration is inconsistent with a Convention-compliant meaning does not of itself make a Convention-compliant interpretation under section 3 impossible. Section 3 enables language to be interpreted restrictively or expansively. But section 3 goes further than this. <u>It is also apt to require a court to read in words which change the meaning of the enacted legislation, so as to make it Convention-compliant. In other words, the intention of Parliament in enacting section 3 was that, to an extent bounded only by what is 'possible', a court can modify the</u>*

---

16 See para 12 of Lord Neuberger's speech *'The role of judges in human rights jurisprudence: a comparison of the Australian and UK experience'* (8 August 2014)– available at https://www.supremecourt.uk/docs/speech-140808.pdf

<u>meaning, and hence the effect, of primary and secondary legislation.</u>"[17] (emphasis added)

57. Elaborating on the point further in the same case, Lord Steyn observed:

> "*Nowhere in our legal system is a literalistic approach more inappropriate than when considering whether a breach of a Convention right may be removed by interpretation under section 3. <u>Section 3 requires a broad approach concentrating, amongst other things, in a purposive way on the importance of the fundamental right involved</u>*"[18] (emphasis added)

58. Later, Lord Rodger opined:

> "*In any given case, however, there may come a point where, standing back, the only proper conclusion is that the scale of what is proposed would go beyond any implication that could possibly be derived from reading the existing legislation in a way that was compatible with the Convention right in question. In that event, the boundary line will have been crossed and only Parliament can effect the necessary change.*"[19]

59. The corollary being that adopting a Convention based analysis allows the court to "read down" the meaning of particular statutory provisions to ensure that existing legislation is read in a way that is that is compatible with convention rights.

60. Saliently, as the ECtHR observed in *Kroon v The Netherlands* (1994) *19 EHRR 263, [1995] 2 FCR 28*:

---

17 Per Lord Nicholls of Birkenhead at para [32]
18 Per Lord Steyn at para [41]
19 Per Lord Rodger at para [115]

> "...Where the existence of a family tie with a child has been established, the State must act in manner calculated to enable that tie to be developed and legal safeguards must be established that render possible as from the moment of birth or as soon as practicable thereafter the child's integration in his family"[20]

And that

> <u>"In the Court's opinion, "respect" for "family life" requires that biological and social reality prevail over legal presumption."</u>[21]
> (emphasis added)

61. As Munby P observed in *Re X*, in *Kroon*, the Strasbourg court accepted that "family life" existed between two parents (and their children) despite the fact that the parents were not married and lived in different houses. The development of this jurisprudential school of thought is captured in this jurisdiction, by Munby J (as he then was) in *Singh v Entry Clearing Officer New Delhi* [2004] EWCA Civ 1075, when his lordship observed:

> "It is also clear that "family life" is not confined to relationships based on marriage or blood, nor indeed is family life confined to formal relationships recognised in law. Thus family life is not confined to married couples. A de facto relationship outside marriage can give rise to family life (Abdulaziz, Cabales and Balkandali v United Kingdom at para [63]), even if the parties do not live together (Kroon v The Netherlands (1994) 19 EHRR 263 at para [30]), and even if the couple consists of a woman and a female-to-male transsexual (X, Y and Z v United Kingdom 1997 24 EHRR 143 at para [37]). So there can be family life between father and child even where the parents are not married: Keegan v Ireland

---

20 *Kroon v The Netherlands (1994) 19 EHRR 263, [1995] 2 FCR 28* at para 32
21 *Supra at para 40*

(1994) 18 EHRR 342 at para [44]. Likewise there can be family life between a parent and a child even where there is no biological relationship: X, Y and Z v United Kingdom at para [37] (family life existed as between the female-to-male transsexual partner of a woman and the child she had conceived by artificial insemination by an anonymous donor).[22]

62. In *A v P (Surrogacy: Parental order: Death of Applicant)* [2011] EWHC 1738 (Fam), Theis J summarised the submissions in relation to the positive obligation under Article 8 on behalf of the applicant and the child [at 30]:

"Following the positive obligation identified by Marck v Belgium the court should seek to ensure that the child is in an equivalent relationship with each parent. The court is therefore seeking to protect the rights to respect to family life of the unit as well as each of the individual members. The rights of the child and his interests have

'…primacy of importance…This is not, it is agreed, a factor of limitless importance in the sense that it will prevail over all other considerations. It is a factor, however, that must rank higher than any other. Where the best interest of the child clearly favour a certain course, that course should be followed unless countervailing reasons of considerable force displace them.' (ZH (Tanzania) v Secretary of State for the Home Department (ibid) per Lord Kerr SCJ para 46).

Only a parental order would have the effect of transforming the legal status of the child such that both commissioning parents are recognised as being the legal parents of the child."

---

22 Per Munby J at para [59]

63. In a subsequent judgment in *A and B (No 2 – Parental Order) [2015] EWHC 2080 (Fam)*, Theis J observed that, *"If de facto family life is established, which it is submitted it is on the facts of this case, then there is a positive obligation to construe statues in a way as to enable them to comply with the Convention [The European Convention on Human Rights]."* [23]

64. The issue arose in *Re A (A child: surrogacy: s54 criteria) [2020] EWHC 1426 (Fam)* where Keehan J was concerned with an application for a parental order where the case presented three legal issues in respect of the parental order application:

    i. that the application is made outside of the 6-month time limit (s54 (3))
    ii. that the child's 'home' at the time of the application and the making of the order (s54(4)(a)), should it be made, will not be the same home as both parents owing to their separation; and
    iii. That at the time of the application, the applicants are two persons who are living as partners in an enduring family relationship as prescribed by s54(2)(c)

65. In *Re A*, 'Keehan J adopted the view that the concept of home must and should be construed flexibly [24] and went on to conclude:

    "The term 'home' must be given a wide and purposive interpretation. The authorities make clear that the term is not and should not be restricted to cases where the applicants live together under the same roof. It is the plain intention of the parents that A will be cared for by both of them, albeit not necessarily, and not at present, on the basis of an equal shared care arrangement. Giving a wide and purposive interpretation

---

23 Per Theis J at para [47]
24 See also Pauffley J in *In KB & RJ v RT* [2016] EWHC 760 (Fam) at para [41]

of the word 'home', I am satisfied that A has his 'home' with the mother and the father.

The father's indirect contact is progressing to direct contact and, in due course, to staying contact. In the premises I shall focus on the parents' agreement in respect of the future care arrangements for A and their joint commitment to be fully involved in his life. I consider that in doing so I am acting in compliance with A's Art 8 and Art 14 rights."[25]

66. A critical point in the facts of *Re A* was that the intended father, had by the time of the hearing for a parental order had not had any direct contact with the child, let alone the child having a physical presence in the intended father's home. This case is therefore a useful example of the extent to which the courts are prepared, so far as it is possible, to interpret the s54 to ensure that a sensible result is achieved.

67. Similarly, in *Re X (Parental order: death of intended parent prior to birth) [2020] EWFC 39*, Theis J was concerned with an application for a parental order with similar issues that arose in *Re A*, namely whether an order could be made under s54(4)(a) in respect of the home of the applicants where one of the intended parents had died and under s54(2)(c) that the application must be made by two people. The case differed to an earlier decision of Theis J – *A v P (Surrogacy: Parental Order: Death of Applicant) [2011] EWHC 1738 (Fam)* – where an intended parent died *after* the application for a parental order was made, but *before* the order was made. In *Re X* one of the intended parents had died prior to the birth of the child, so before an application could even be made, which would clearly present an issue in respect of the 'home' requirement. The application was complicated further because the surviving intended parent's gametes were not used to create the embryo

---

25 Per Keehan J at para [58]-[59]

and therefore she would not be able to apply for a single parental order, which would not, in any event, be consistent with the child's life-story.

68. Theis J identified 5 reasons why the court was able to conclude that Parliament intended that in circumstances where an intended father dies after the embryo transfer but prior to the child's birth should not be "barred forever" from making an application for parental order. Theis J observed:

> *"(1) As in Re X, Parliament has not explained its thinking why such a situation is excluded, when but for Mr Y's death prior to the birth all the requirements under s 54 would have been met following X's birth. There is no reason to believe Parliament either foresaw or intended the potential injustice which would result in this case if a parental order cannot be made in the circumstances in this case.*
>
> *(2) Other provisions in the HFEA 2008 (ss 35 – 37) provide clarity about the status of the father of the child born as a result of assisted conception at the time when the embryo is transferred, or artificial insemination takes place, provided certain safeguards are in place, in particular consent. Consent is not an issue in this case, any consent required by s 54 is present and secure.*
>
> *(3) The provisions set out in ss 39 and 49 HFEA provide clarity as to the status of the father in the circumstances of sub-paragraph (2) where they take place after his death, again with safeguards in place relating to consent.*
>
> *(4) Parliament has recently, when considering the declaration of incompatibility made by the court in Re Z (No 2), signalled that it seeks to ensure that the law does not discriminate against different categories of applicants for parental orders on the grounds of relationship status.*

(5) A parental order is the only route by which X can have her status regarding Mr and Mrs Y recognised in a way that was intended by the surrogacy arrangement, which a parental order was specifically created for."[26]

69. Theis J was fortified in the conclusion she had reached above on the basis that Convention rights were engaged. Theis J went on to identify no fewer than nine reasons which supported that conclusion:

(1) Both Articles 8 and 14 are engaged.

(2) Munby P foreshadowed at paragraph 61 in Re X a situation such as this, when he highlighted the part of Article 8 that protects 'private life'; as he stated there may be cases where it may be more difficult to establish 'family life'. Here X did not have the opportunity to establish 'family life' due to the premature death of Mr Y, but X certainly has an established 'private life' right for her own identity to be protected by legal recognition of her relationship with Mr Y. The court's responsibility is to 'guarantee not rights that are theoretical and illusory but rights that are practical and effective' (Marckx v Belgium (1979 – 80) 2 EHRR 330 at paragraph 31). As Russell J observed in Re A and B [2015] EWHC 911 at paragraphs 62 – 63:

> *"62. It is undeniably a basic and fundamental part of these children's identity as human beings that the Applicant/father is their biological father, and that the Applicant/mother played a full part in the process of their conception having selected an egg donor, as she has herself explained to them and as they have grown up believing. The Applicants were their planned and intended parents from before conception and since the*

---

26 Per Theis J at para [93]

day on which they were born. All of these facts, fundamental to these children's very existence and identity are far from those present in adoption. Again I quote from the President's judgment in Re X; "Adoption is not an attractive solution given the commissioning father's existing biological relationship with X. As X's guardian puts it, a parental order presents the optimum legal and psychological solution for X and is preferable to an adoption order because it confirms the important legal, practical and psychological reality of X's identity; the commissioning father is his biological father and all parties intended from the outset that the commissioning parents should be his legal parents."

63. To make adoption orders would effectively deny adequate recognition of the Applicants' and children's identity and their right to family life under Article 8 ECHR, particularly their established identity, their biological and social ties. There is no doubt in this case that as far as these children are concerned their identity has already been formed as the biological children of their father and the commissioning of their conception and birth involving their mother."

(3) Although I have concluded that Parliament cannot have intended that a child in X's position would be excluded from such recognition, without the 'reading down' required by s 3 the provisions s 54 (1), (2) (a) (4) (a) and (5) could prevent a parental order being made.

(4) From the extensive review set out above it is clear such a reading down does not go against the 'grain of the legislation', on the contrary it seeks to provide the order that it is accepted best meets a child born as a result of this type of arrangement.

The parental order was specifically created for a child born as a result of a surrogacy arrangement, such as in this case.

(5) No alternative order that can properly and accurately to reflect X's identity, including her relationship with Mr Y. A child arrangement or special guardianship order in favour of Mrs Y would mean Mrs Y secures parental responsibility limited to X's minority, but such an order would not negate X's legal relationship with Mr and Mrs Z, and would result in her biological father remaining a legal stranger to X. Mrs Y could apply for an adoption order, but only as a single applicant, which may give her the status of a legal parent but it will not accurately reflect X's identity in relation to either Mr or Mrs Y. This route would create something of a legal fiction, as s 67 ACA states that the effect of an adoption order is the adopted person is to be treated in law as if born as a child of the adopter, which does not reflect the reality of the surrogacy arrangement entered into. In addition, such a course could have a distorting effect as Mrs A would be an adoptive parent, the register would be marked that way and the tracing of the child's natural parents is still done in the same way as for any other adopted child.

(6) For X her connection with her biological father would be safeguarded in any other birth circumstances naturally or by way of assisted conception, consequently it is discriminatory for the circumstances of her birth to prevent this. A failure of the law to recognise her connection with her biological father as the result of her birth through a surrogacy arrangement amounts to a breach of her Article 14 right to enjoy her Article 8 rights without discrimination on the grounds of birth.

(7) Mrs Y's article 14 rights are also engaged. She is discriminated against based on her relationship status as a widow,

rather than being married. In Re Z (No 2) Munby P stated at paragraph 17

> *"Sections 54(1) and (2) of the Human Fertilisation and Embryology Act 2008 are incompatible with the rights of the Applicant and the Second Respondent under Article 14 ECHR taken in conjunction with Article 8 insofar as they prevent the Applicant from obtaining a parental order on the sole ground of his status as a single person as opposed to being part of a couple."*
>
> *(8) The consequences of not making a parental order in this case is that there is no legal relationship between X and her biological father; X is denied the social and emotional benefits of recognition of that relationship; X may be financially disadvantaged if there is not legal recognition as the child of her biological father; X does not have a legal reality that matches the day-to-day reality; X is further disadvantaged by the death of her biological father.*
>
> *(9) The only order that will confer joint and equal parenthood on Mr and Mrs Y is a parental order. Only that order will ensure X's security and identity in a lifelong way respecting both her Article 8 and 14 rights.*
>
> *It is clear that reading down the provisions in s 54 (1), (2) (a), (4) (a) and (5) in this case to permit the parental order to be made would not be incompatible with the 'underlying thrust of the legislation being construed' and the words sought to be implied 'go with the grain of the legislation'. The HFEA sought to provide a comprehensive legal framework for those undertaking assisted conception, with the aim of securing the rights of any child born as a result. That policy and legislative aim remains intact if the order sought in this case is made."*

70. Like the *Re X* decided by Munby P regarding the parental order application time limit, Theis J's decision in the recently decided *Re X* is of profound importance in illustrating the extent to which the court is prepared to go to ensure that a parental order can be made. It also re-asserts the importance of Convention based principles.

At the time of the application and the making of the order, either or both of the applicants must be domiciled in the UK or in the Channel Islands or the Isle of Man s54(4)(b);

71. The law in relation to domicile is well established. An individual is said to have *domicile of origin* from birth. They will be said to be domiciled in that country unless and until they abandon that and acquire a *domicile of choice* in another jurisdiction.

72. In respect of domicile of origin, in the case of *Re Fuld* [1967] 3 All ER 318, Scarman J (as he then was) opined:

> "(1) The domicile of origin adheres unless displaced by satisfactory evidence of the acquisition and continuance of a domicile of choice; (2) a domicile of choice is acquired only if it is affirmatively shown that the propositus is resident in a territory subject to a distinctive legal system with the intention, formed independently of external pressures, of residing there indefinitely. <u>If a man intends to return to the land of his birth upon a clearly foreseen and reasonably anticipated contingency, e.g., the end of his job, the intention required by law is lacking; but, if he has in mind only a vague possibility, such as making a fortune (a modern example might be winning a football pool), or some sentiment about dying in the land of his fathers, such a state of mind is consistent with the intention required by law.</u> But no clear line can be drawn; the ultimate decision in each case is one of fact - of the weight to be attached to the various factors and future contingencies in the

contemplation of the propositus, their importance to him, and the probability, in his assessment, of the contingencies he has in contemplation being transformed into actualities. (3) <u>It follows that, though a man has left the territory of his domicile of origin with the intention of never returning, though he be resident in a new territory, yet if his mind be not made up or evidence be lacking or unsatisfactory as to what is his state of mind, his domicile of origin adheres....</u>" (emphasis added)

73. The proposition to be extracted from *Re Fuld* is that there must be clear evidence that an individual's domicile of origin has been displaced. The acquisition of a new domicile of choice is a serious matter. In *Mark v Mark [2005] UKHL 42*, Lady Hale observed that *"English law requires only that the intention [of the person claiming to be domiciled by reason of their intention to reside permanently in the UK] be bona fide, in the sense of being genuine and not pretended for some other purpose..."*[27]

74. In *Barlow Clowes International Limited v Henwood [2008] EWCA Civ 577*, Arden LJ (as she then was) observed:

   "Given that a person can only have one domicile at any one time for the same purpose, he must in my judgment have a <u>singular and distinctive relationship with the country of supposed domicile of choice. That means it must be his ultimate home</u> or, as it has been put, the place where he would wish to spend his last days". (emphasis added) "[28]

75. Arden LJ went on to observe:

   "First, as Lord Macnaghten said in Winans, the courts should not too readily find that a person has lost his domicile of origin because a change of domicile affects a person's status. At 294,

---

27 Per Lady Hale, at para [47]
28 Per Arden LJ, at para [14]

Lord Macnaghten quoted with approval observations of Lord Cranworth and Lord Wensleydale in Whicker v Hume (1858) 10 HLC 124 to the effect that "in these days, when the tendency of the educated and leisured classes is to become cosmopolitan — if I may use the word- you must look very narrowly into the nature of the residence suggested as a domicil (sic) of choice before you deprive a private man of his native domicil (sic).

It is difficult with respect to see why this reason does not equally apply to loss of a domicile of choice. ***In an increasingly cosmopolitan world, where migration is not confined to higher socio-economic groups and travel and communication is much easier, it is likely that many people will be as attached to a domicile of choice they have acquired as to a domicile of origin which they enjoyed originally. The law should reflect that fact.*** *(emphasis added)*

Secondly, it is said that as a practical matter it is easier to establish that the domicile of origin has been retained because it is associated with a person's native character and thus presumably in most cases it can be inferred that he would have wanted that domicile. ...

But that second rationale does not apply universally. ....[The learned judge gives examples of situations where a person may have a limited attachment to his/her country of origin]

It seems to me that as a general proposition the acquisition of any new domicile should in general always be treated as a serious allegation because of its serious consequences. None of the authorities cited to us preclude that approach, and such an approach ensures logical consistency between two situations

> where the policy interest to be protected is (as demonstrated above) the same. ..."²⁹

76. In the context of a surrogacy case concerning domicile, 10 factors were identified by Theis J in *Z v C (Parental Order: Domicile) [2011] EWHC 3181 (Fam)*, adopting the approach taken by Arden LJ in *Barlow Clowes International Limited*:

   i. *A person is, in general, domiciled in the country in which he is considered by English law to have his permanent home. A person may sometimes be domiciled in a country although he does not have his permanent home in it.*

   ii. *No person can be without a domicile.*

   iii. *No person can at the same time for the same purpose have more than one domicile.*

   iv. *An existing domicile is presumed to continue until it is proved that a new domicile has been acquired.*

   v. *Every person receives at birth a domicile of origin.*

   vi. *Every independent person can acquire a domicile of choice by the combination of residence and an intention of permanent or indefinite residence, but not otherwise.*

   vii. *Any circumstance that is evidence of a person's residence, or of his intention to reside permanently or indefinitely in a country, must be considered in determining whether he has acquired a domicile of choice.*

   viii. *In determining whether a person intends to reside permanently or indefinitely, the court may have regard to the motive for*

---

29 Per Arden LJ at para [90]-[94]

which residence was taken up, the fact that residence was not freely chosen, and the fact that residence was precarious.

ix. *A person abandons a domicile of choice in a country by ceasing to reside there and by ceasing to intend to reside there permanently, or indefinitely, and not otherwise. A person who has formed the intention of leaving a country does not cease to have his home in it until he acts according to that intention.*

When a domicile of choice is abandoned, a new domicile of choice may be acquired, but if it is not acquired, the domicile of origin revives[30]

77. Where there is a question of domicile in respect of a parental order application, either that an intended parent is asserting they have not relinquished their domicile of origin despite not living in the UK or conversely, that they have acquired domicile of choice here, despite being born elsewhere, it will always be a question of fact that the court will have to determine on written, and sometimes oral evidence.

The applicants must be over 18 at the time of the making of the order s54(5);

78. Of all of the s54 criteria, the requirement that the intended parent(s) be over 18 is probably the criteria yet to face challenge in court, perhaps because it is a simple question of fact that can be proved with ease.

---

30 Per Theis J at para [13]

The court must be satisfied that the surrogate (and her husband if applicable) freely, and with full understanding of what is involved, have agreed unconditionally to the making of an order s54(6);

79. Consent is the bedrock that underpins the way in which the statutory framework operates when concerned with a parental order application. As the statute stipulates, it requires the surrogate and her husband, if applicable, to consent unconditionally to the making of a parental order. Consent is obtained by the surrogate signing Form A101A. 'Agreement to the making of a parental order in respect of my child'"[31]. In England and Wales, the form must be witnessed by an officer of the Children and Family Court Advisory and Support Service (Cafcass) or, where the child is ordinarily resident in Wales, by a Welsh family proceedings officer. If the surrogate does not live in England and Wales then it is customary for it to be signed by the surrogate and endorsed by a notary, or equivalent in that jurisdiction.

80. Saliently, by s54(7) of the HFEA 2008 consent is only deemed valid, if it is given six weeks *after* the birth of the child.

81. The A101A form states:

> *I agree to a parental order being made in respect of _____ (my child), who is the child to whom the attached certified copy of the entry in the Register of Live Births relates. in favour of*
>
> *[_____
> __(the named prospective parents)]*

---

[31] https://www.gov.uk/government/publications/form-a101a-agreement-to-the-making-of-a-parental-order-in-respect-of-my-child-section-54-of-the-human-fertilisation-and-embryology-act-2008

If a parental order is made in respect of my child, I understand that I will no longer legally be treated as the parent and that my child will become part of the family of the applicant(s).

I understand that I may withdraw my agreement at any time until the court makes the parental order. If I do withdraw my agreement and want my child returned to me, I understand that I must notify the court that I have changed my mind and I must, at all times, act through the court and not approach the applicants directly.

I have not received any payment or reward from any person making arrangements for the parental order for my child.

*[I have taken legal advice] / *[I have not taken legal advice, but I have been advised to do so],
about giving agreement to a parental order being made in respect of my child and the effect on my parental rights.
*(delete as appropriate)

I agree unconditionally and with full understanding of what is involved, to the making of a parental order in respect of

_____
_____ (my child) in favour of
*[_____
__(the applicant(s)]

82. In cases of multiple birth, an A101A form must be completed and signed for each child – i.e. where a surrogate is married and gave birth to twins, there will four forms completed.

83. There have been a number of cases where the issue of consent has arisen – namely in cases where consent from the surrogate (and her husband) has not been forthcoming. Unlike cases of adoption, where a court has the power to dispense with a birth

parents' consent to a child being placed for adoption if the welfare of the child requires the court to do so[32], no such provision exists under the HFEA 2008. The court's power to dispense with consent in respect of a parental order is limited to circumstances where the surrogate cannot be found or is incapable of giving agreement under s54(7) of the HFEA 2008 (discussed further below).

84. In *Re AB (Surrogacy: Consent) [2016] EWHC 2643 (Fam)*, Theis J was concerned with a domestic surrogacy arrangement. The intended parents, C and D, were the biological parents of the twins, A and B, who were born in 2015. The respondents were E and F, the surrogate and her husband. Post birth, relations between the surrogate, her husband and the intended parents became strained and whilst the twins had been placed in the care of the intended parents, the surrogate and her husband did not consent to the making of a parental order.

85. Apart from the requirement under s54(6), all of the other criteria were met. However, as Theis J observed what was "*.. perhaps so unusual about this case is, as set out above, the respondents wish to take no part in the children's lives. Their rationale for refusing their consent is due to their own feelings of injustice, rather than what is in the children's best interests."*[33]

86. The stark reality when consent is not forthcoming was summarised thus by Theis J

> "Without the respondent's consent the application for a parental order comes to a juddering halt, to the very great distress of the applicants. The result is that these children are left in a legal limbo, where, contrary to what was agreed by the parties at the time of the arrangement, the respondents will remain

---

32 Adoption and Children Act 2002 s52(1)(b)
33 Per Theis J at para [8]

their legal parents even though they are not biologically related to them and they expressly wish to play no part in the children's lives."[34]

87. Whilst the surrogate and her husband were unwilling to consent to the making of a parental order, they were willing to consent to the making of an adoption order in respect of the twins. Such an order would see the intended parents, both of whom were biologically related to the twins, adopt their own genetic children which would not reflect the twins' social reality and their individual life stories in circumstances where an adoption order has the effect of treating the children as if they were the children of the intended parents, which they already were.[35]

88. Theis J concluded the case by adjourning the application for a parental order generally, giving the parties the option of restoring the matter (i.e. rather than having dismissed the application) in the event that there was a change in the parties' position, with the twins remaining the subject of a child arrangements order. In favour of the intended parents.

89. The court's ability to dispense with the surrogate's consent to the making of a parental order if that is consistent with the welfare needs of the child is something being considered by the Law Commission in their review on the law related to surrogacy. However, it seems unlikely that any new proposals to dispense with the surrogate's consent could operate retrospectively, in circumstances when the time at which the surrogate entered into the surrogacy arrangement, her ability to freely withhold her consent was a key part of the basis upon which she entered into that arrangement. *Prima facie*, this

---

34 Per Theis J at para [9]
35 See *In the matter of the HFEA 2008 (Cases A, B, C, D, E, F, G and H Declaration of Parentage)* [2015] EWHC 2602 (Fam) at para [71]

would be retrospectively moving the 'goal posts'. In situations like the *Re AB* case, the only real route to acquiring legal parenthood would be an adoption order, where the intended parents are already social and genetic parents, despite adoption not being consistent with the children's life story.

90. In *H (a child: surrogacy breakdown) [2017] EWCA Civ 1798* the Court of Appeal was concerned with an appeal where a same sex male couple entered into a surrogacy arrangement with a surrogate and her husband. The parties' relationship broke down and communication ceased. After the birth, the solicitors representing the surrogate and her husband, wrote to the intended parents to inform them that they no longer wished to follow the terms of their agreement and would not be providing their consent to the making of a parental order. Unable to make a parental order, the court at first instance made a number of orders under s8 of the Children Act 1989 to regularise the child's status with the intended parents and restrict the surrogate and her husband from being able to exercise parental responsibility. The surrogate and her husband appealed, arguing that the trial judge had made a parental order in all but name. The Court of Appeal upheld the trial judge's decision.

91. The Court of Appeal endorsed the words of the trial judge (Theis J)

> *"This case is another example of the complex consequences that can arise from entering into this type of arrangement. Even though C was an experienced surrogate, this case demonstrates the risks involved when parties reach agreement to conceive a child which, if it goes wrong, can cause huge distress to all concerned. For all the adults involved, who all clearly love H, the one thing I know they will agree is that their dispute and this contested litigation has been a harrowing experience for them all. This case is another example of the consequences of not*

having a properly supported and regulated framework to underpin arrangements of this kind."[36]

92. Given the central importance of consent to the making of a parental order and the court's inability to adopt a different approach in interpreting the statue to make a parental order, it means that where the requirement is not met, the court will be required to adopt a creative approach to the types or orders that are made that are within the court's power. This issue is discussed more in Chapter 8.

S54(7) – Where the surrogate is incapable of being found

93. In cases where s54(7) is engaged and the court is being invited to dispense with the surrogate's consent because she cannot be found, the court will exercise extreme cation before doing so. In *Re D and L (Surrogacy)* [2012] EWHC 2631 (Fam), Baker J (as he then was) said this in respect of dispensing with consent:

> *"It is a very important element of the surrogacy law in this country that a parental order should normally only be made with the consent of the woman who carried and gave birth to the child. The reasons for this provision are obvious. A surrogate mother is not merely a cipher. She plays the most important role in bringing the child into the world. She is a 'natural parent' of the child. As Baroness Hale of Richmond observed in Re G (Children) [2006] UKHL 43 at paragraphs 33-35."*

And that:

> *"The act of carrying and giving birth to a baby establishes a relationship with the child which is one of the most important relationships in life. It is therefore not surprising that some sur-*

---

36 See *H (a child: surrogacy breakdown)* [2017] EWCA Civ 1798 at para [27]

rogate mothers find it impossible to part with their babies and give consent to the parental order. That is why the law requires that a period of six weeks must elapse before a valid consent to a parental order can be given."[37]

94. Baker J went on to find that three matters must be undertaken by a court when a court is invited to dispense with consent:

> *"First, when it is said that the woman who gave birth to the child cannot be found, the court must carefully scrutinise the evidence as to the efforts which have been taken to find her. It is only when all reasonable steps have been taken to locate her without success that a court is likely to dispense with the need for valid consent. Half-hearted or token attempts to find the surrogate will not be enough. Furthermore, it will normally be prudent for the Applicants to lay the ground for satisfying these requirements at an early stage. Even where, as in this case, the Applicants do not meet the surrogate, they should establish clear lines of communication with her, preferably not simply through one person or agency, and should ensure that the surrogate is made aware during the pregnancy that she will be required to give consent six weeks after the birth.*
>
> *Secondly, although a consent given before the expiry of six weeks after birth is not valid for the purposes of section 54, the court is entitled to take into account evidence that the woman did give consent at earlier times to giving up the baby. The weight attached to such earlier consent is, however, likely to be limited. The courts must be careful not to use such evidence to undermine the legal requirement that a consent is only valid if given after six weeks.*
>
> *Thirdly, in the light of the changes affected by the 2010 regulations, the child's welfare is now the paramount consideration*

---

[37] Per Baker J at para [25]-[26]

when the court is 'coming to a decision' in relation to the making of a parental order. Mr Ford submits, and I accept, that this includes decisions about whether to make an order without the consent of the woman who gave birth in circumstances in which she cannot be found or is incapable of giving consent. It would, however, be wrong to utilise this provision as a means of avoiding the need to take all reasonable steps to attain the woman's consent." [38]

95. As with other criteria under s54, it will be an evidential question for the court to be satisfied that reasonable steps have been taken to identify the whereabouts of the surrogate as opposed to "half-hearted" or "token" attempts to locate the surrogate. In *R and S v T (Surrogacy: Service, Consent and Payments) [2015] EWFC 22* the applicants for a parental order, following a surrogacy arrangement in the Ukraine, invited Theis J to dispense with the surrogate's consent as she was unable to be located. In that case the applicants had taken a number of steps to identify the surrogate's location including seeking the clinic's consent to provide details of the surrogate's whereabouts which they refused.

96. Part 13 of the Family Procedure Rules 2010. (FPR. 2010) requires the respondent (i.e the surrogate) to be served with the application for s parental order. Rule 13.6 provides that (1) The applicants must, within 14 days before the hearing or first directions hearing, serve on the respondents, a) the application, b) a form acknowledging service; and c) a notice of proceedings. This provision is particularly relevant when dealing with cases concerning a surrogate who is unable to be located. Theis J concluded in *R and S v T (Surrogacy: Service, Consent and Payments)* that whilst there was no specific provision that gives the court power to dispense with service of the application on the respondent, the court, nevertheless, has the power to do so.

---

38 Per Baker J at para [28]-[30]

Theis J was satisfied that there were general powers in rule 13.9(1)(f) where the court could give directions about tracing the surrogate and service of documents, together with rule 4.1(3)(o) which provides that the court may *"take any further step or make any other order for the purpose of managing the case and furthering the overriding objective"*.

97. Theis J concluded that she was satisfied that the applicants had taken all reasonable steps to locate the surrogate and was therefore content to dispense with the surrogate's consent to the making of a parental order.

> *The court must be satisfied that no money or other benefit (other than for expenses reasonably incurred) has been given or received by either of the applicants for or in consideration of (a)the making of the order, (b)any agreement required by subsection (6), (c)the handing over of the child to the applicants, or (d)the making of arrangements with a view to the making of the order – s54(8).*

98. The provisions of s54(8) are mandatory. As to whether payments go beyond reasonable expenses is fact specific, but it is plain that it would be contrary to the spirit of s54(8) to endorse payments that were disproportionate.

99. As discussed further below, the changes facilitated by the Human Fertilisation and Embryology (Parental Orders) Regulations 2010, the lifelong welfare of the child is paramount and the court must balance that with public policy considerations, with arguably more weight being placed on welfare.

100. In *Re X and Y (Foreign Surrogacy) [2008] EWHC 3030 (Fam)* Hedley J observed:

> "In relation to the public policy issues, the cases in effect suggest (and I agree) that the court poses itself three questions:
>
> i. was the sum paid disproportionate to reasonable expenses?
> ii. were the applicants acting in good faith and without 'moral taint' in their dealings with the surrogate mother?
> iii. were the applicants' party to any attempt to defraud the authorities?"[39]

101. In 2010, the impact of the implementation of the HFEA 2008 and its associated regulations was highlighted, again by Hedley J, in *Re L (a minor) [2010] EWHC 3146 (Fam)* with respect to welfare being the court's paramount consideration:

> "What has changed, however, is that welfare is no longer merely the court's first consideration but becomes its paramount consideration. The effect of that must be to weight the balance between public policy considerations and welfare (as considered in Re X and Y) decisively in favour of welfare. <u>It must follow that it will only be in the clearest case of the abuse of public policy that the court will be able to withhold an order if otherwise welfare considerations supports its making</u>... I think it important to emphasise that, notwithstanding the paramountcy of welfare, the court should continue carefully to scrutinise applications for authorisation under Section 54(8) with a view to policing the public policy matters identified in Re S (supra) and that it should be known that that will be so."
> [40](emphasis added)

102. In *Re WT [2014] EWHC 1303 (Fam)*, Theis J opined:

---

39 Per Hedley J at para [21]
40 Per Hedley J at para [10]

"When considering whether to authorise the payments made in this case the relevant principles are firmly established by the cases, starting with Re X and Y (Foreign Surrogacy) [2008] EWHC 3030 (Fam) [2009] 2WLR 1274 (paragraph 19 and 20) and the cases that have followed (in particular Re S (Parental Order) [2009] EWHC 2977 (Fam), Re L (Commercial surrogacy) [2010] EWHC 3146 (Fam), [2011] 2WLR 1006 Re IJ (Foreign Surrogacy Agreement Parental Order) [2011] EWHC 921 (Fam) [2011] 2FLR 646 and Re X and Y (Parental Order: retrospective authorisation of paymwnts) [2011] EWHC 3147 (Fam)

(1) the question whether a sum paid is disproportionate to "reasonable expenses" is a question of fact in each case. What the court will be considering is whether the sum is so low that it may unfairly exploit the surrogate mother, or so high that it may place undue pressure on her with the risk, in either scenario, that it may overbear her free will;

(2) the principles underpinning section 54 (8), which must be respected by the court, is that it is contrary to public policy to sanction excessive payments that effectively amount to buying children from overseas.

(3) however, as a result of the changes brought about by the Human Fertilisation and Embryology (Parental Orders) Regulations 2010, the decision whether to authorise payments retrospectively is a decision relating to a parental order and in making that decision, the court must regard the child's welfare as the paramount consideration.

(4) as a consequence it is difficult to imagine a set of circumstances in which, by the time an application for a parental order comes to court, the welfare of any child, particularly a foreign child, would not be gravely compromised

by a refusal to make the order: As a result: "it will only be in the clearest case of the abuse of public policy that the court will be able to withhold an order if otherwise welfare considerations support its making", per Hedley J in Re L (Commercial Surrogacy) [2010] EWHC 3146 (Fam), [2011] 2WLR 1006, at paragraph 10.

(5) where the applicants for a parental order are acting in good faith and without 'moral taint' in their dealings with the surrogate mother, with no attempt to defraud the authorities, and the payments are not so disproportionate that the granting of parental orders would be an affront to public policy, it will ordinarily be appropriate for the court to exercise its discretion to give retrospective authorisation, having regard to the paramountcy of the child's lifelong welfare.

103. In *A, B and C (UK Surrogacy expenses)* [2016] EWFC 33, Russell J observed that:

"It remains necessary for the court to consider matters of public policy set out above in considering whether to exercise the power of authorisation under s54(8) HFEA 2008, but the court should only refuse a parental order in the "clearest case of the abuse of public policy". The approach developed by Hedley J has subsequently been endorsed by Theis J in A v P [2011] EWHC 1738 (Fam) and by Sir Nicholas Wall, the President of the Family Division, in Re X (children) [2011] EWHC 3147 (Fam).

The need for the court to consider issues of public policy extends to welfare and to ensure that commercial surrogacy agreements are not used to circumvent childcare laws in this country, resulting in the approval of arrangements in favour of people who would not have been approved as parents on welfare grounds under any set of existing law such as adoption. To

> *paraphrase Hedley J, the court must be careful not to be involved in anything that looks like a payment for buying. Such arrangements have been ruled out by Parliament and the court cannot be party to any arrangements which effectively allow them."* [41]

104. The authorities make it clear that a parental order should only be refused in the *"clearest case of the abuse of public policy"*. The court will be obliged ask itself whether the sum paid to the surrogate will have overborne her capacity to freely consent to the making of a parental order. In *A, B and C (UK Surrogacy expenses) [2016] EWFC 33*, Russell J shed much needed clarity to the often held misconception as to whether there was a fixed sum as to what would amount to reasonable expenses, observing that *"There is no universally acceptable figure to pay for surrogacy expenses in the UK irrespective of the circumstances in law.."* [42]

105. Whilst commercial surrogacy is prohibited in this jurisdiction, a court making a parental order has the power to retrospectively authorise payments that are not reasonably incurred. This is a task that is undertaken regularly in international cases, the court recognising that commercial surrogacy is a lawful and profit-making enterprise in other jurisdictions.

106. In *Re P-M (Parental Order: Payments to Surrogacy Agency) [2014] 1 FLR 724* Theis J made clear that the court's scrutiny should include payments that are made to agencies who are acting on a commercial basis and therefore inevitably there will be element of profit.

107. Where a commercial surrogacy arrangement has been entered in another country where it is lawfully permitted, it is only possible to seek authorisation of commercial payments after the

---

41 Per Russell J at para [28]-[29]
42 Per Russell J at para [3]

event (i.e. during the parental order process). Authorisation of such payments is therefore separate to expenses that have been incurred reasonably.

Welfare

108. Welfare is not a specific criteria under s54 of the HFEA 2008. However, The Human Fertilisation and Embryology (Parental Orders) Regulations 2010 must be read in conjunction with the s54 criteria and came into force in April 2010. Paragraph 2 and schedule 1 of the Regulations apply s1 of the Adoption and Children Act 2002 to parental order applications so that the child's welfare must be the court's *"paramount consideration... throughout his lifetime"*.

109. The effect of this provision is that s1 of the Adoption and Children Act 2002 applies to the making of a parental order in the following terms:

> *"(1) This section applies whenever a court is coming to a decision relating to the making of a parental order in relation to a child.*
>
> *(2) The paramount consideration of the court must be the child's welfare, throughout his life.*
>
> *(3) The court must at all times bear in mind that, in general, any delay in coming to the decision is likely to prejudice the child's welfare.*
>
> *(4) The court must have regard to the following matters:*
>
>> *a) the child's ascertainable wishes and feelings regarding the decision (conceived in the light of the child's age and understanding),*

> *b) the child's particular needs,*
>
> *c) the likely effect on the child throughout his life, of having ceased to be a member of the original family and become the subject of a parental order,*
>
> *d) the child's age, sex, background and any infant child's characteristics which the court considers relevant,*
>
> *e) any harm (within the meaning of the Children Act 1989) which the child has suffered or is at risk of suffering,*
>
> *f) the relationship which the child has with relatives, and with any other person in relation to whom the court considered the relationship to be relevant.*

110. The significant impact that welfare considerations have on parental order applications can be best seen in the context of when public policy considerations arise concerning the authorisation of payments made to surrogates. Hedley J made this clear in *Re L (a minor)* discussed above, that the balance is tipped decisively in favour of welfare and that only on the clearest case of abuse of public policy would the court decline to make a parental order.

Conclusion

111. The cases discussed in this chapter illustrate that the statutory requirements for the making of a parental order are, to a certain extent, open to challenge. However, there remain elements of the statutory criteria where if the criteria cannot be satisfied it is a bar to a parental order being made (e.g. consent of the surrogate). Ultimately, this chapter highlights that when entertaining an application for a parental order, welfare will

always be the courts lodestar. The next chapter will examine the welfare principle in greater detail.

CHAPTER FIVE
WELFARE

1. As discussed in preceding chapters, the welfare of the child who is the subject of a parental order application is paramount. The Human Fertilisation and Embryology (Parental Orders) Regulations 2010 and section 1 of the Adoption and Children Act 2002 are the starting point when having regard to welfare.

2. Section 1 of the Adoption and Children Act 2002 contains the welfare checklist that is read in a similar fashion to the checklist contained on s1 of the Children Act 1989, however a significant difference imported by the 2002 Act is that the court is obliged to have regard to the child's welfare *throughout* their lifetime as opposed to until they reach adulthood at 18. This is particularly significant in cases of surrogacy. The "transformative" nature of a parental order, similar to that of an adoption order in terms of transfer of legal parentage, means that the court has an important balancing exercise to consider – i.e. if an order is not made, what impact will that have, not just on the child now, but throughout their entire lifetime. It is a consideration of magnetic importance that cannot be overstated.

3. Section 1(4) of the Adoption and Children Act 2002 states:

   (4) The court or adoption agency must have regard to the following matters (among others)—

   (a) the child's ascertainable wishes and feelings regarding the decision (considered in the light of the child's age and understanding),

   (b) the child's particular needs,

(c) the likely effect on the child (throughout his life) of having ceased to be a member of the original family and become an adopted person,

(d) the child's age, sex, background and any of the child's characteristics which the court or agency considers relevant,

(e) any harm (within the meaning of the Children Act 1989 (c. 41)) which the child has suffered or is at risk of suffering,

(f) the relationship which the child has with relatives, with any person who is a prospective adopter with whom the child is placed, and with any other person in relation to whom the court or agency considers the relationship to be relevant, including—

(i) the likelihood of any such relationship continuing and the value to the child of its doing so,

(ii) the ability and willingness of any of the child's relatives, or of any such person, to provide the child with a secure environment in which the child can develop, and otherwise to meet the child's needs,

(iii) the wishes and feelings of any of the child's relatives, or of any such person, regarding the child.

4. In cases where there are public policy considerations, welfare often tips the balance in favour of a court granting a parental order. Speaking extra-judicially, Hedley J said this:

> "The statute does give power to the High Court retrospectively to authorise these payments and the reason we do so is not because we want to encourage commercial surrogacy but because of the impossible position which the child born as a result of the arrangement finds themselves in when they're back in this country"

> *"Commercial surrogacy is a highly controversial matter ethically and at the end of the day by the time the case gets to me **the best I can normally do is to focus on the welfare of the child**... If that means that the will of Parliament has been subverted, well that is, I think, a matter Parliament will have to address"* (emphasis added)[1]

5. The observations of Hedley J highlight the ambivalence that judges have, where they might be viewed as driving a coach and horses through the fabric of our unwritten constitution and the general principle of separation of powers were they to attempt to subvert the will of Parliament.

Assessing welfare: Life story work

6. A significant and profound part of the assessment of welfare involves a social work concept called "life story" work. The concept is traditionally used in cases where a child is placed for adoption or when a child is received into local authority care, as a tool for the child to understand why they do not live with their birth parents. With surrogacy, the concept is helpful, and whilst there is a significant difference in that the child born via a surrogacy arrangement has not been removed from their birth family (i.e. parental orders *reflect* parenthood as it was intended and adoption orders *replace* parenthood), there are, themes that resonate with children born via surrogacy.

7. A prominent school of thought that has developed over the last few decades by researchers examining children who have been placed for adoption is that not being truthful about a child's history- i.e. their conception and birth history -can risk under-

---

[1] Hedley J speaking to the BBC Radio 4's The World at One, 19 May 2011. See also https://www.bbc.co.uk/news/uk-13452330 'High Court judge approves commercial surrogacy'

mining trust in families and that a transparent and honest approach between parents and children encourages stronger relationships. The same can be said about children born via surrogacy, particularly in the case where donor gametes have been used.

8. Until relatively recently, the majority of parents who gave birth to donor-conceived children did not intend to tell their children about their genetic origins. Many parents express a concern that if their children were aware of their genetic origins the children would be left confused, upset or shocked that they were not genetically related to one parent.[2]

9. In 2013, The Nuffield Council on Bioethics, in their report 'Donor Conception: ethical aspects of information sharing' took the view that openness about a child's conception has a positive impact on the quality of relationships for families as well as for the well-being of those families.[3]

10. The Nuffield Council report echoes the sentiments of research undertaken by Professor Susan Golombok, a professor of family research and director of the Centre for Family Research at the University of Cambridge. Professor Golombok's research in relation to donor conceived children says this about secrecy where gamete donation has been used to create a family is highly contentious. Research in respect of adopted children where secrecy has occurred has illustrated that some children may develop emotional, behavioural and identity problems; and that there is a direct parallel in donor-conceived families where secrecy is deployed.[4]

---

2 See Golombok, S 'Modern Families: parents and children in new family forms' (2015) Cambridge Univeristy Press
3 Available at https://www.nuffieldbioethics.org/publications/donor-conception
4 See Golombok, S 'Modern Families: parents and children in new family forms' (2015) Cambridge University Press at page 93-95

11. Professor Golombok's extensive research in this area highlights why it is necessary for the court to have regard to the child's *lifelong* welfare, given the psychological implications that are at play with respect to donor conceived children.

12. Ultimately it is a matter for the intended parents how they wish to address this issue of profound importance, however the overwhelming message from contemporary research is that transparency is key. Moreover, it is exactly the kind of issue that a parental order reporter during the course of their enquiries would likely wish to discuss with intended parents. With same sex couples, preparing a narrative to assist with a child's life story is much easier in circumstances where it is going to be fairly clear to an outside observer and indeed the child. The opposite is sometimes the case with opposite sex couples who may wish to conduct their family life in a way that is not consistent with the child's life story, which may lead to some of the difficulties in later life as described by Professor Golombok in her research.

13. Organisations such as the Donor Conception Network have a host of resources that are essential reading and offer advice on how best to approach the subject of telling a child about their origins when donor gametes have been used.

Donor conceived children and identity

14. Whilst there is no hard and fast rule on the approach that should be taken by intended parents in relation to donor conceived children, these issues engage principles that are fundamental to Article 8 (right to private and family life) of the European Convention on Human Rights. The European Court of Human Rights (ECtHR) has emphasised repeatedly that the breadth of Article 8 includes a child's right to know their

origins. In the case of *Mennesson v France* (Application No. 65192/11), a case concerning recognition of a Californian surrogacy arrangement in France, the ECtHR observed that *"respect for private life requires that everyone should be able to establish details of their identity as individual human beings, which includes the legal parent-child relationship."*[5].

15. The approach taken by the ECtHR in *Godelli v Italy (Application no. 33783/09)* in the context of adoption and parentage is a helpful case that illustrates the balance that domestic courts must seek to achieve between the competing interests of the parent and those of the child. The applicant in *Godelli* was a child who was abandoned at birth. Under Italian law it was lawful for the birth mother to relinquish the child without her name being recorded on the birth certificate. The applicant subsequently discovered she was adopted (when she was 10) and sought information about her birth mother. The domestic court dismissed the relief sought by the applicant. The applicant took the case to the ECtHR on the basis that there was an interference with her Article 8 rights afforded under the ECHR and that she was entitled to know who her birth parent was under Article 7 of the UN Convention on Rights of the Child. The court observed that: "The Court must examine whether a fair balance has been struck in the present case between the competing interests: on the one hand, the applicant's right to have access to information about her origins and, on the other, the mother's right to remain anonymous."[6] The Court concluded that the Italian authorities had failed to strike a balance and "achieve proportionality between the interests at stake and thus overstepped the margin of appreciation which it must be afforded."[7]

---

5 At para [96]
6 Godelli at para [47]
7 Godelli at para [58]

16. Subsequent caselaw, particularly in the context of paternal DNA testing (for example, *Jaggi v Switzerland* (2008) 47 E.H.R.R. 3052), demonstrates the ECtHR giving more weight to the right of knowing one's origins. Plainly there are differences in the context of DNA paternity testing where there might be a dispute about parentage, but there remains a fundamental point in relation to identity and the importance for a child to know about their genetic heritage. [8]

17. In short, there is an established principle that can be taken from Article 8: that respect for private life requires that individuals should be able to establish details of their identity, which should not be obstructed without specific justification for doing so.[9] The most obvious example is in relation to specific medical conditions, such a mitochondrial disorders which can only be inherited from a mother and therefore in cases where a donor egg was used and an intended mother had a particular mitochondrial disorder, a child who became cognisant of their mother's mitochondrial condition, may, unnecessarily, start to question whether they are at risk of the same condition.

18. All of these issues are important considerations that anyone going through the parental order process must consider. More importantly, and aside from the growing European and domestic jurisprudence about the right to know the truth about an individual's genetic heritage, longitudinal studies in relation to donor conceived families show that openness from the outset allows donor conceived children to integrate it as part of their identity. The opposite is true if information is concealed. Overall, research also suggests from longitudinal studies that there is more positive functioning in families where transparency about conception is adopted.[10]

---

8 See also *In the matter of TT and YY* [2019] EWHC 2384 (Fam)
9 See also *Gaskin v United Kingdom* (Application no. 10454/83) at para [39]

Examining the welfare principle

19. Each application for a parental order must consider welfare, and so the issue is examined in all of the cases to which this book has referred, although not always explicitly.

20. One aspect where welfare plays an important role, is the intended parents' parenting capacity with respect to age. Whilst section 54 has a minimum age limit there is not a maximum age limit. The relevance with respect to welfare may occur in cases where the intended parents are older and the parental order reporter and/ or the court expresses concern about the impact making such an order will have.

21. In *R v T [2015] EWFC 22*, the applicants in this case were in their early sixties, and had been married for 38 years. They spent many years trying to conceive a child; when the female applicant was in her early forties, they had IVF treatment. Following a number of IVF procedures, both in the UK and abroad, they were advised to consider surrogacy. In examining the welfare principle, Theis J relied heavily on the observations of the parental order reporter. Theis J observed:

> *42. Turning to welfare the court's paramount consideration is each of the children's lifelong welfare needs. The court has the benefit of the two reports prepared by Mr McGavin, an experienced member of the Cafcass High Court Team. He recommends parental orders are made in relation to both children. He discussed the applicants' health with them and was satisfied by the responses made. The applicants have reported in their written evidence that neither has any health concerns. One of the matters Mr McGavin rightly raises in his report is the need for the applicants to make satisfactory*

---

10 See Golombok, S 'Modern Families: parents and children in new family forms' (2015) Cambridge University Press at page 115-116

> *arrangements, in the event that they are unable to care for the children. At the hearing I was informed by Ms Cabeza that those arrangements are in hand, all relevant documents are drafted, the male applicant's niece has agreed to be a testamentary guardian and these arrangements will be implemented once the parental orders are made.*
>
> *43. It is quite clear that each of these children require the position with their current carers to be secured in a way that provides lifelong security. That will reflect the position in their country of birth, where the applicants are their legal parents. If the parental order is not made the surrogate mother will remain, as a matter of English law, the legal mother of these children in circumstances where there is no realistic prospect of her having any future role in the children's lives. Their de facto parents are the applicants, their lifelong welfare interests are best served if that reality is reflected in their legal relationship with the applicants. Mr McGavin reports 'When I visited them [the children] appeared content and well cared for babies whose physical and emotional needs are being well met by [the applicants] who are entirely delighted to have them. They are much loved and anticipated children.'*
>
> *44. The lifelong welfare needs of each of these children require the court to make parental orders which is the order I shall make.*[11]

22. Similar issues arose in *Re C (A Child) (Parental Order) [2013] EWHC 2413 (Fam)*. Theis J granted a parental order in relation to a child conceived with the intended father's sperm, and eggs from an anonymous Russian donor, using a married Russian surrogate mother. The court authorised a compensation payment to the surrogate representing one to two years' average

---

11 Per Theis J paras [42]-[44]

wages and the retention by the arranging agency of a sum representing approximately half the fee paid.

23. When considering the welfare aspects of the case, the court made the following observations in relation to some of the concerns raised by the parental order reporter:

> *33. The parental order reporter conducted a full assessment into the welfare aspects of this case. The Second Applicant has three grown up children from her first marriage, who in turn have twelve children between them. The parental order reporter raised with the Applicants the mature age of the Second Applicant and what plans they had made to ensure C's continued care if she became ill or died. The First Applicant made it clear he was prepared and available to continue to parent C. The parental order reporter also discussed this with the Second Applicant's daughter, who has her own children. She confirmed she spoke to her mother each day, and although she lived some way away she had plans to move closer. She was clear that she would do everything she could to support C in the event that he lost his mother during his childhood.*
>
> *34. Although the Applicants now have parental responsibility by virtue of the residence order made by the court at the first hearing they are not C's legal parents and C lacks a lifelong connection with the Applicants for matters as significant as inheritance, financial support and his wider identity. Without an order he would be left in something of a legal vacuum, without full legal membership of any family anywhere in the world.*
>
> *35. Following her extensive and comprehensive enquires the parental order reporter concluded.*

> "53. C's permanent home will be with [the Applicants]. A parental order will benefit all members of the family as it will secure C in law as the applicants' child and the extended family members will be reassured about his future. This will afford all of them the greatest possible security.
>
> *36. I agree. His welfare needs would clearly not be met by the Respondents remaining his legal parents in this jurisdiction, when they are not so recognised in their own jurisdiction and have no intention of having any future parental role in C's life. <u>C's future is in the long term care of the Applicants, they are his de facto legal parents and his welfare demands their relationship is given lifelong security which can only be achieved by making a parental order.</u>*[12] *(*emphasis added)

24. In both of these cases the issues of the age of the intended parents has been raised or touched upon by the parental order reporter. However, in reality, in the absence of their being major public policy concerns, or a criteria of the s54 criteria *not* being met that is not capable of being 'read down' (e.g. domicile) that would vitiate the court's ability to make a parental order, it is difficult to envisage a set of circumstances where a court would refuse to make a parental order without welfare tipping the balance.

25. In *Re C (A Child) (Parental Order and Child Arrangement Order) [2020] EWHC 2141* Keehan J granted a parental order and child arrangements order following the intended parents' separation. The facts of the case bear setting out given the unique facts involved. The court was concerned with C who was aged 2 years old, born as a result of a surrogacy arrangement made in X country. A donor egg was used and together with the intended father's gametes an embryo was created. Following

---

12 Per Theis J para [33]-[36]

earlier proceedings, C was living with his father. Despite the parties' separation, they jointly applied for a parental order in respect of C.

26. A key feature to the background of the case was that the intended mother signed a second surrogacy agreement without the father's consent. Twins were born as a result of the second surrogacy arrangement. They remained living in X country with the intended mother or alternate carers until they arrived in the UK with the mother in 2020. In an earlier fact finding hearing, the court had made a number of adverse findings about the intended mother's credibility.[13] In addition to this, Keehan J found that the intended father had not consented to the extension of the period of storage of his genetic material by the surrogacy agency in X country and that the intended father did not consent to the second surrogacy arrangement. Notwithstanding the issues that arose in the case Keehan J concluded that he was *"wholly satisfied that it is in the welfare best interest of C"*[14] that a parental order be made in favour of the intended parents.

27. Critically, the court gave permission for an expert psychologist to be instructed to undertake work about how C should be told about the existence of the half twin siblings.

Conclusion

28. Welfare forms an essential ingredient when looking at applications for parental orders, particularly having regard to the transformative nature of parental orders. Welfare also plays a critical role in cases where it is not possible for a parental order to be made and the court has to look to other legal routes to

---

13 *Re C (A Child: Parental Order & Child Arrangements Order)* (17 April 2020)
14 Per Keehan J at para [109]

securing a legal relationship to the child and the intended parents.

CHAPTER SIX
THE PARENTAL ORDER REPORTER AND THEIR DUTIES

1. The parental order reporter plays a key role in the parental order application process.

2. Upon the making of an application for a parental order, the court will direct that CAFCASS (the Children and Family Court Advisory and Support Service) appoint a parental order reporter. The role of the parental order reporter is to consider the best interests of the child and investigate the circumstances of the case with respect to the s54 HFEA 2008 criteria. As qualified and experienced social workers, the parental order reporter plays a vital role in addressing the matters concerning welfare.

3. In *Z (Children: foreign surrogacy: allocation of work: guidance on parental order reports) [2015] EWFC 90* Russell J encapsulated that the role of the parental order reporter is to:

    "Investigate the matters set out in s.54(1) to (8) of the 2008 Act, as required under the Family Procedure Rule 16.352A, and to do so in accordance with para.10.1 of the Practice Direction 16A which gives further directions as to how those investigations are to be carried out, including that the Parental Order reporter 'should contact or seek to interview such persons as the Parental Order reporter thinks appropriate, or the court directs'"[1]

---

1 Per Russell J at para [88]

4. The relevant procedure and rules in respect of parental order reports are contained in part 16 of Family Procedure Rules 2010, which states:

> *16.35 Powers and duties of the parental order reporter*
>
> *16.35.—(1) The parental order reporter is to act on behalf of the child upon the hearing of any application in proceedings to which Part 13 applies with the duty of safeguarding the interests of the child.*
>
> *(2) The parental order reporter must—*
>
> *(a) investigate the matters set out in sections 54(1) to (8) of the 2008 Act;*
>
> *(b) so far as the parental order reporter considers necessary, investigate any matter contained in the application form or other matter which appears relevant to the making of the parental order; and*
>
> *(c) advise the court on whether there is any reason under section 1 of the 2002 Act (as applied with modifications by the Human Fertilisation and Embryology (Parental Orders) Regulations 2010) to refuse the parental order.*
>
> *(3) The parental order reporter must also provide the court with such other assistance as it may require.*
>
> *(4) The parental order reporter's duties must be exercised in accordance with Practice Direction 16A.*
>
> *(5) A report to the court by the parental order reporter is confidential.*

5. Further guidance relating to the role of parental order reports is contained in Practice Direction PD16A which states:

> *Practice Direction PD 16A*
>
> *10.1 The parental order reporter must make such investigations as are necessary to carry out the parental order reporter's duties and must, in particular –*
>
> *(a) contact or seek to interview such persons as the parental order reporter thinks appropriate or as the court directs; and*
>
> *(b) obtain such professional assistance as is available which the parental order reporter thinks appropriate or which the court directs be obtained.*
>
> *How the parental order reporter exercises duties – attendance at court, advice to the court and reports*
>
> *10.2 The parental order reporter must attend all directions hearings unless the court directs otherwise.*
>
> *10.3 The parental order reporter must advise the court on the following matters –*
>
> *(a) the appropriate forum for the proceedings;*
>
> *(b) the appropriate timing of the proceedings or any part of them;*
>
> *(c) the options available to it in respect of the child and the suitability of each such option including what order should be made in determining the application; and*

(d) any other matter on which the court seeks advice or on which the parental order reporter considers that the court should be informed.

10.4 The advice given under paragraph 10.3 may, subject to any direction of the court, be given orally or in writing. If the advice is given orally, a note of it must be taken by the court or the court officer.

10.5 The parental order reporter must –

(a) unless the court directs otherwise, file a written report advising on the interests of the child in accordance with the timetable set by the court; and

(b) where practicable, notify any person the joining of whom as a party to those proceedings would be likely, in the opinion of the parental order reporter, to safeguard the interests of the child, of the court's power to join that person as a party under rule 13.3 and must inform the court –

(i) of any notification;

(ii) of anyone whom the parental order reporter attempted to notify under this paragraph but was unable to contact; and

(iii) of anyone whom the parental order reporter believes may wish to be joined to the proceedings

6. The parental order reporter provides assistance to the parental order application process by way of a written report of their observations, views and recommendations (i.e. whether the court should make a parental order, or perhaps identifying further evidence that might be required to comply with a particular criteria under s54).

7. Prior to the COVID-19 pandemic, there was debate as to whether it was a mandatory requirement for the parental order reporter to physically see the child with the intended parents. In *Re Z*, Russell J observed:

> *"It is the view and guidance of this court that the Parental Order reporter's investigation in any case must include the child being seen with the applicant unless there are compelling and exceptional reasons based on the child's welfare why such observations cannot take place, or where there is sufficient independent evidence pertaining to the child's welfare from an alternative source."*[2]

8. However, in *AB (Foreign Surrogacy – children out of the jurisdiction) [2019] EWFC 22*, Theis J was concerned with an application for a parental order in respect of children who were not present in the jurisdiction at the time of the final hearing. In this case Theis J considered the circumstances in which the court could make a parental order when the subject children were not physically present in the jurisdiction. The applicants for the parental order were A and B. Both were born and married in Iran and came to the UK as a result of A being at risk because of his political views. B subsequently secured British citizenship and A was granted unlimited leave to remain in the UK.

9. A surrogacy arrangement took place in Iran using A's gametes. The surrogate gave birth in 2017 and A's biological connection with the children was confirmed with DNA testing. Following the children's birth, B flew to Iran. From then until December 2018 (save for one week in June) one or other of the applicants was located in Iran to be able to help care for the children. The children were based with the wider family. Both applicants

---

2   Per Russell J in *Z (Children: foreign surrogacy: allocation of work: guidance on parental order reports) [2015] EFWC 90* at para [86]

registered the birth in Iran with their names on the birth certificate.

10. Theis J was satisfied on the evidence available to the court that the guidance from *Re Z* had been followed and that the parental order reporter (who was also the children's guardian, the children having been joined to the proceedings) had had sufficient opportunity to see the children with the applicants via two Skype video calls.

11. Before making parental orders, Theis J granted a time-limited adjournment to enable the Secretary of State for the Home Department (SSHD) to be given notice of the application and for time for any representations that the SSHD wished to make. The SSHD was given notice and did not wish to make any representations and parental orders were made shortly thereafter.

12. During the COVID-19 pandemic, parental order applications continued via remote means, with hearings being conducted remotely and parental order reporters undertaking their enquiries and assessments using video call technology. It is not clear whether this will become more of a regular occurrence in the future and that there will be an expectation of parental order reports to undertake their work in person. However, given the justice system's rapid response to the public health emergency in 2020, and the use of modern technology that allowed proceedings to continue, legal arguments over what may amount to "exceptional reasons" based on a child's welfare may well be expanded, with something like a public health emergency being an acceptable reason for a parental order reporter not to meet the child in person.

13. In exceptional and complex cases, sometimes the child who is the subject of the parental order application, might be joined to

the proceedings as a party. In such circumstances part 16 or the Family Procedure Rules 2010 applies and the individual who has been appointed as the parental order reporter is generally appointed as the child's guardian as well.

CHAPTER SEVEN
THE PARENTAL ORDER APPLICATION PROCESS

1. Part 13 of the Family Procedure deals with proceedings under s54 of the HFEA 2008. It is of course axiomatic that Part 13 must be read in conjunction with other parts of the FPR in relation to making applications. This chapter will deal with the application process and give a general overview of the relevant family procedure rules.

2. The application is made on a C51 'Application for a parental order: Section 54 or 54A of the Human Fertilisation and Embryology Act 2008'. An application form must be completed for each child, even if it is the same respondents. The form is readily available online.[1]

3. Below is a summary of the key points from the 2010 Family Procedure Rules.[2]

Who are the parties – FPR 13.3

4. The intended parents will always be the applicants to an application for a parental order where they can satisfy the conditions set out in section 54(1) of the HFEA 2008 (i.e. an application that is made by either a husband and wife, civil partners or two persons who are living as partners in an enduring family relationship). Where the application is made under section 54A, the single intended parent will be the sole applicant.

---

1 https://assets.publishing.service.gov.uk/government/uploads/system/uploads/attachment_data/file/790489/c51-eng.pdf
2 https://www.justice.gov.uk/courts/procedure-rules/family/parts/part_13#IDAZLOIC

5. The respondents to an application for a parental order will always be the woman who carried the child (i.e. the surrogate) and the other parent (if any) if the surrogate is married. Rule 13.3 also provides that any other person in whose favour there is a provision for contact and any other person or body (i.e. a local authority) with parental responsibility for the child at the date of the application. The court also has the power to direct that a person with parental responsibility for the child be made a party to the proceedings where that person requests such status.

6. Within rule 13.3 there are also broad powers for the court to direct that any other person or body be made a respondent to the proceedings – as well as removing respondents from the proceedings. In circumstances where the court makes a direction for the addition or removal of a party it should also give consequential directions about serving a copy of the application form on any new respondent, serving relevant documents on the new party and management of the proceedings.

Notice of proceedings to a person with foreign parental responsibility – FPR. 13.4

7. By rule 13.4, a person who holds or is believed to hold parental responsibility for the child under the law of another State which exists in accordance with Article 16 of the 1996 Hague Convention, following the child becoming habitually resident in a territorial unit of the UK, that person is not required to be joined as a respondent under rule 13.3. Where such persons are identified, the applicant shall give notice to those individuals (rule 13.4(2)).

8. Rule 13.4(3) also provides for the applicant and all respondents to the proceedings to provide any details that they possess as to the identity and whereabouts of any other person they believe to hold parental responsibility for the child.

What happens once the application issued? – FPR 13.5

9. The application is issued at the applicants' local family court (allocation of proceedings will be discussed further below). Once issued the court will:

    a) Set a date for the first directions hearing;
    b) Appoint a parental order reporter;
    c) Set a date for the final hearing of the application;
    d) The court office will return to the applicants the copies of the application together with any other documents that the applicant is required to serve; and send a certified copy of the entry in the register of live births to the parental order reporter.

Service of the application and other documents – FPR 13.6

10. The applicants must, within 14 days before the hearing or the first directions hearing, serve on the respondents:

    a) The application;
    b) A form for acknowledging service; and
    c) A notice of proceedings.

11. Finally, the applicants must serve a notice of proceedings on any local authority or voluntary organisations that has at any time provided accommodation for the child.

Acknowledgement – FPR 13.7

12. Within 7 days of the service of an application for a parental order, each respondent must file an acknowledgment of service and serve it on the other parties.

Date of the first directions hearing – FPR 13.8

13. Unless the court directs otherwise, the first directions hearing must be within 4 weeks from when the application was issued.

The first directions hearing – FPR 13.9

14. At the first directions hearing in the proceedings the court will:

    a) Set a timetable for the filing of:
        i. Any report from the parental order reporter;
        ii. If a statement of facts has been filed, any amended statement of facts; and;
        iii. Any other evidence;
    b) Give directions relating to the report of the parental order reporter and other evidence;
    c) Consider whether any other person should be a party to the proceedings, and if so, give directions in accordance with FPR 13.3(3) or (4) by joining that person as a party to the proceedings;
    d) Give directions relating to the appointment of a litigation friend for any protected party unless a litigation friend has already been appointed;
    e) Consider (in accordance with rule 291.17 – 'transfer of proceedings') whether the case needs to be transferred to another court and; if so give appropriate directions;
    f) Give directions about
        i. tracing the other part or the woman who carried the child;
        ii. Service of the documents;

iii. Disclosure as soon as possible of information and evidence to the parties. (subject to rule 13.12);

iv. The final hearing;

15. The parties or their legal representatives must attend the first directions hearing unless the court directs otherwise. Directions may be given at any stage of the proceedings, of the court's own initiative or on the application of a party or the parental order reporter.

Where the agreement of the other parent or woman who carried the child is not required – FPR 13.10

16. Section (54(7) of the HFEA 2008 deals with circumstances where the surrogate's consent cannot be obtained because she is incapable of being found. In such cases rule 13.10 is relevant, as well as the guidance set out by Baker J in *Re D and L (Surrogacy) [2012] EWHC 2631* discussed in chapter 4. In such cases, the applicant's must:

   a) State that the agreement is not required in the application form, or any later stage in writing to the court;

   b) File a statement of facts setting out a summary of the history of the case any other facts to satisfy the court that the other parent or woman who carried the child cannot be found or is incapable of giving agreement;

Agreement – FPR 13.11

17. Consent to the making of a parental order is dealt primarily in section 54(6) of the HFEA 2008. Rule 13.11 provides for how the consent must be obtained. The agreement is obtained by the surrogate (and her husband – i.e. the other parent – if applicable) signing the Form A101A, unless the court directs otherwise. The following rules apply:

a) In Scotland any form of agreement must be witnessed by a Justice of the Peace of a Sheriff;

b) In Northern Ireland any form of agreement must be witnessed by a Justice of the Peace;

c) In England and Wales, agreement in the A101A from must be witnessed by an officer of the Children and Family Court Advisory and Support Service (Cafcass) or, where the child is ordinarily resident in Wales, by a Welsh family proceedings officer.

d) Where the form of agreement is executed outside of the UK, it must be witnessed by any person authorised by law in that country to administer an oath for any judicial or other legal purpose; a British Consular officer; a notary public; or if the person executing the document is serving in any of the regular armed forces of the Crown, an officer holding a commission in any of those forces.

Reports of the parental order reporter and disclosure to the parties – FPR. 13.12

18. By this rule, the court has the power to consider whether to give a direction that a confidential report of the parental order be disclosed to each party to the proceedings. In circumstances where the court is minded to do so, the court will consider whether any information should be deleted or redacted. The court has the power to direct that the parental order report is not disclosed to any party. It is sensible to raise this issue at the first hearing when the court directs the date for filing of the parental order report, for there to be permission for the report to be served. on the applicants as well.

The final hearing – FPR 13.13- 13.14

19. The court officer will give notice to the parties and to the parental order reporter of the date and place where the application is to be heard. Any person given notice of the final hearing may attend and may be heard on the question of whether an order should be made

Proof of identity of the child – FPR 13.15

20. The court will deem the child referred to in the application as the child referred to in the form of agreement (i.e. the form A101A). The following conditions must be met:

    a) the application identifies the child by reference to a full certified copy of an entry in the registers of live births;

    b) the form of agreement identifies the child by reference to a full certified copy of an entry in the registers of live births attached to the form; and

    c) the copy of the entry in the registers of live-births referred to above is the same or relates to the same entry in the registers of live-births as the copy of the entry in the registers of live-births attached to the form of agreement.

Orders – FPR 13.20

21. The parental order takes effect from the date when it is made, or such later date as the court may specify.

Copies of Orders. – FPR 13.21

22. Within 7 days, from the date of the parental order was made (or a shorter time the court may direct) a court officer is responsible sending:

a) A copy of the order to the applicant;

b) A sealed copy authenticated with a stamp of the court (or certificated as a true copy of a parental order) to the Registrar General;

c) A notice of the making or refusal of:

   i. The final order; or

   ii. An order quashing or revoking a parental order or allowing an appeal against an order in proceedings, to every respondent and, with the permission of the court, any other person

d) The court officer will also send notice of the making of a parental order to:

   i. any court in Great Britain which appears to the court officer to have made any such order as is referred to in section 46(2) of the Adoption and Children Act 2002 (order relating to parental responsibility for, and maintenance of, the child); and

   ii. the principal registry, if it appears to the court officer that a parental responsibility agreement has been recorded at the principal registry.

e) A copy of any final order may be sent to any other person with the permission of the court.

f) The court officer will send a copy of any order made during the course of the proceedings to all the parties to those proceedings unless the court directs otherwise

Allocation of domestic and international cases (England and Wales only)

23. Where the surrogacy arrangement has taken place in England and Wales (i.e. the child was born in England and Wales), those applications are usually heard by magistrates sitting in the Family Court where the application was made. However, if there are legal issues concerning interpretation of the section 54 HFEA 2008 criteria, then such matters are likely to be heard in the High Court.

24. The court timetable in terms of case management follows the process set out in the Family Procedure Rules.

25. As with all family law applications, it is incumbent on all parties (particularly in domestic applications heard in lower courts) to identify at the earliest possible stage whether there are issues of a complex nature that should be allocated to a more senior judge. Such cases will usually be cases where one or more of the s54 criteria of the HFEA 2008 are in issue.

26. Where the application for a parental order concerns an international surrogacy arrangement and the child was born abroad, such cases are automatically allocated to the High Court. Whilst the application is usually made at the Central Family Court, in cases with an international element, it is an administrative process and the application is automatically allocated to the High Court on paper.

27. As discussed in the earlier chapter concerning the role of the parental order reporter, in *Re Z (Foreign Surrogacy: Allocation of Work: Guidance on Parental Order Reports) [2015] EWFC 90*, Russell J also comprehensibly set out guidance on allocation, which was approved by the then President of the Family Division, Munby P. Her ladyship observed:

> "71. Parental order applications of overseas surrogacy or those with an international element, particularly those where the children were born outside the jurisdiction as a result of a surrogacy agreement whether it was commercial or not invariably involve some legal complexity. As Mrs Justice Theis said in CC and DD [2014] EWHC 1307 (Fam) a case in which the applicants were resident overseas;
>
>> "3. This case highlights once more the legal complexities in this area of the law and the need for those who embark on international surrogacy arrangements to ensure they have expert advice both here and in the jurisdiction where the arrangement is taking place. This international flavour of this case was not unusual: the applicants are of British and French origin, the child was born in the US to a US surrogate mother in an arrangement that involved legal procedures between two US States, the family currently live in France and the proceedings for a parental order are here....
>>
>> 20. There is no requirement under s54 that the applicant or that the child should be present in this jurisdiction. The court's jurisdiction to make a parental rests (sic) *solely on the requirement in s54(4)(b) that at least one of the Applicants has a domicile in a part of the United Kingdom, Channel Islands or the Isle of Man*. As noted above, s54 (4) (a) requires the child's home to be with the applicants at the time of the application and the making of the order, but does not specify that the child's or the applicants home must be in the UK. A parental order is not a Part 1 Order as defined in Chapter I of the Family Law Act 1986 and therefore jurisdiction to make such an order is not governed by that Act.

In this case it was unfortunate that it was not until April 2015 that specialist advice was obtained.

72. *Those representing the Applicants and the children submitted in their joint statement of issues that the "welfare issues raised by this case are stark, serious and exceptional. This travel problem is now resolved. However, absent such solution, it is the parties' submission that in this exceptional case the paramount welfare considerations would also have justified the Court arranging an expeditious consideration of the section 54 considerations so as to allow the making of the parental order. This would have included the court hearing directly from the official in the Passport Office, coupled with an urgent invitation to the Home Office to intervene should it choose to do so. In that way the court could have properly addressed, with representatives of the relevant authorities either present or electing not to be present, the public policy concerns which the course advocated by the parties raise." It can be seen from the case law referred to in this judgment that this case is not particularly exceptional in the experience of the judges in the Family Division who have built up a specialist knowledge and expertise in this area of law and an early listing before a specialist tribunal as is envisaged by the guidelines set out below and approved by the President of the Family Division. Indeed it was submitted on behalf of Cafcass Legal as advocate to the court "that [the proposition that] these proceedings should have been transferred to the High Court and the children made parties to the proceedings at the earliest opportunity seems overwhelming."*

73. <u>*Guidance*</u> *In respect of the allocation of parental order applications there will be the following guidelines applied in keeping with the practice and procedure as set out in Schedule 1, 3 (f) (iv) of the Distribution of Business in the High Court of the Senior Courts Act 1981, rule13.9 (1) (e) of the Family*

Procedure Rules (FPR) 2010 and Schedule 1 paragraph 4(f) of the Family Court (Composition and Distribution of Business) Rules 2014 which have been in force from 22 April 2014 on the formation of the Family Court (as referred to above).

i) All proceedings for parental orders will commence in the Family Court where they will remain. They should not be transferred to the High Court.

ii) All proceedings pursuant to s 54 of the HFEA 2008 where the child's place of birth was outside of England and Wales should be allocated to be heard by a Judge of High Court Level.

iii) In London all cases should, if possible, be allocated to Mrs Justice Pauffley, Mrs Justice Theis or Ms Justice Russell.

iv) Cases which originate on circuit, unless transferred to London, should be allocated to be heard locally by a High Court Judge identified by the Family Division Liaison Judge in consultation with the Judge in Charge of the HFEA list (this is Mrs Justice Theis).

v) Allocation of the case to either the Cafcass High Court Team or to a local Cafcass or Cafcass Cymru officer to act as parental order reporter is a matter for Cafcass (subject to their own guidance and the guidance below).

The first directions hearing

28. In many ways the first directions is much like a case management or first appointment, where the aim of the hearing is, so far as it is practicable, to timetable the matter through to a final hearing. Below is a list of questions that any applicant

should bear in mind when preparing for the first directions hearing.

a) Joinder – does the child need to be joined as a party?

b) Joinder of any other relevant party

c) Evidence required to satisfy the s54 criteria.

d) Expert evidence – does the court need any particular expertise to assist with the parental order application?

Joinder of the child

29. Joining the child as a party to the proceedings follows the same rules prescribed by part 16 of the Family Procedure Rules 2010. Only in the most complex of cases will it be necessary for the child to be joined (e.g. where the child remains abroad, where the surrogate does not consent to the making of a parental order or where there are public policy issues and the court is concerned about possible exploitation in another country.

30. Other cases where it might be necessary for the child to be a party are cases where the parental order application has been made outside of the time limit and/or where the applicants have separated. Joinder should also be considered in cases where the court is being invited to read down a particular part of the s54 criteria or a government body has been joined as an intervener or where there is an application for a declaration of incompatibly.

31. Where a child is joined as a party, the appointed parental order reporter is usually directed to act as the child's guardian as well.

Joinder of any other relevant party (including interveners)

32. The Family Procedure Rules 2010 set above contemplate that it might be necessary to join other parties to the parental order application. For example, in *Re C (A Child) (Parental Order and Child Arrangement Order) – Fact Finding Judgment and Welfare Judgment [2020] EWHC 2141* the local authority were granted permission to intervene where the local authority had was involved with the subject child (incidentally, the child had also been joined as a party in those proceedings). Where a local authority issues proceeding pursuant to s31 of the Children Act 1989 for a care or supervision order and there is still an extant parental order application to be determined, consideration will need to be given as to whether the parental order proceedings should be consolidated with the s31 proceedings, or whether the two sets of proceedings should run concurrently.

Evidence to satisfy the s54 criteria

33. Written evidence in the form of a statement forms the focal point of the applicants' case. Historically there has been something of a mixed approach as to whether there should be a single joint statement from both applicants (in joint applications) or whether each should do a statement, perhaps with one being the main statement and the other endorsing the contents of the other. The most appropriate approach is the latter, with two statements being filed.

34. The main statement in support of the application should address the parties' history, and their journey to parenthood. The main body of the statement should focus on the s54 HFEA 2008 criteria and where possible exhibit evidence in support for the particular provision. For example, in cases where domicile of choice is being asserted, it would be appropriate to exhibit as much documentary evidence as possible that supported that

contention (e.g. bank statements, details of property ownership, citizenship documents etc).

Expert evidence

35. In international cases, particularly in jurisdictions where there might be concerns about exploitation or vulnerable surrogates, written evidence from the applicants should address the due diligence that the applicants undertook when researching their surrogacy options and how they took the decision to instruct X agency or Y clinic. Furthermore, in jurisdictions where surrogacy is seen as an "emerging market" and the legal framework is likely to be unknown about what the status is of the surrogate, the court may also wish to have expert legal evidence about the status of the child in that jurisdiction before it goes on to make a final parental order. Plainly any requirement for expert evidence will need to satisfy part 25 of the Family Procedure Rules 2010, i.e. that an expert report is necessary.

36. In domestic cases, if any of these issues arise, allocation of the case to more senior judge should be considered as early as possible.

The final hearing

37. At a final hearing, depending on the issues, oral evidence is sometimes heard from applicants. In cases where domicile is an issue, the court is likely going to wish to hear from the relevant applicant. Similarly, where the court is invited to make a finding about a particular issue (e.g. whether a relationship is an enduring family relationship) or where public policy issues are engaged, oral evidence is likely to be required.

38. It is unlikely that a court will require oral evidence where all of the s54 criteria re met without any difficulty.

39. Drawing from a tradition that has been established in the Family Court in adoption proceedings, where a court grants a parental order, there is sometimes an opportunity for a 'celebration hearing' either immediately at the conclusion of the parental order final hearing, or at a later date. During these short hearings there is sometimes an opportunity for a photograph with the child and the intended parents in the courtroom (sometimes with the judge or magistrates too if they are so inclined). For many intended parents this forms part of the child's life story work, with many intended parents seeing it as an essential part of the child's understanding of their identity.

Withdrawing from proceedings

40. There are few cases that set out the procedure for withdrawing for an application for a parental order. However, in *Z and Y (Leave to Withdraw Application for a Parental Order) [2019] EWFC 43* Theis J was confronted with an unusual application in parental orders proceedings where the applicants sought the court's permission to withdraw their application for a parental order. Following a number of adjourned interim hearings, the applicants filed a statement in January 2019 setting out the evidence they relied upon to establish how they met the conditions under s54 of the HFEA 2008. At a further interim hearing in March 2019, the court directed a further information to be filed that was relevant to two of the s54 criteria: the consent of the surrogate and payments made by the applicants. Following that hearing, the applicants emailed the court and the parental order reporter, indicating that they felt strongly that the court should have made a parental order on the information already before the court, and as a result they had decided not to continue with their application.

41. The children were joined as a party to the proceedings, with the parental order reporter becoming their guardian. Attempts were made by the guardian to try and re-engage the applicants, but to no avail. The applicants remained steadfast in their wish to withdraw from the proceedings, and sent a further email to the court and the children's guardian confirming their wish to withdraw.

42. At the adjourned hearing in June 2019 the applicants did not attend. Theis J set out options that were available to the court:

    a) Adjourn the application to a fixed date to see if the applicants could be further encouraged to participate in their application;

    b) Adjourn the application generally with liberty to restore;

    c) Make the parental order;

    d) Give permission for the applicants to withdraw their application

43. Her ladyship considered each of the options. The guardian supported the applicants' application for leave to withdraw from proceedings in circumstances where the court could not properly satisfy itself that the s54 criteria were met - despite it being contrary to the welfare needs of the children. Allowing the applicants permission to withdraw, Theis J observed "*By taking the position they have they have risked the children's lifelong welfare needs being met by pursuing their application*"[3]

44. The bigger picture that this case illustrates that where there are significant evidential gaps to establish the s54 criteria, there is only so far the court can go. In circumstances where there is a real paucity evidence (for whatever reason) the court will not be

---

3   Per Theis J at para [21]

able to make an order, notwithstanding the transformative effect a parental order has on the status of children born via surrogacy.

45. The case also highlighted issues regarding parental responsibility. There was a 'lives with' child arrangements order that afforded both parents with parental responsibility by virtue of s12 of the Children Act 1989. However, the court went on to make a free-standing parental order under s4 of the Children Act 1989 but *only* in respect of the father (because he was the genetic father and therefore a parental responsibility order under s4 of the Children Act 1989 can only be made in respect of a parent). Theis J went on to observe that:

> *"Ms Y cannot have such an order as her parental responsibility arises only from the child arrangements order, as the surrogate remains the legal mother. This means, as a matter of law, her parental responsibility could be said to be more precarious as it would be discharged automatically on the discharge of the child arrangements order. Whereas parental responsibility under s 4 can only be discharged by an application to the court or the making of an order that affects status, such as an adoption order. As Ms Carew submits there is no difference to the quality of the parental responsibility, but an order under section 4 is a status independent of any other order, such as the child arrangements order."*[4]

46. For the children in this case, there remains, as Theis J observed "limitations" on the parents' legal relationship with the children. Such limitations include the status of the children following the death of the parents in terms of inheritance, particularly in circumstances where the parents had an older child who was conceived naturally and therefore had a different status to that of the children born through surrogacy, unless and until a parental order is made.

---

4   Per Theis J at para [23]

Revocation of parental orders

47. Revocation of a parental order is rare, and a similar approach is taken by the court when entertaining revocation of an adoption order given the similarities in the status they afford. Hedley J confirmed this approach in *G v G [2012] EWHC 1979 (Fam)*. In *G v G* the application to revoke arose following the intended father's application to revoke, where he alleged that the intended mother had concealed her true intentions at the time of the order being made (that she wanted to live alone with the child and not as a family unit). The intended father contended that had those matters been known at the time, he would not have applied for a joint parental order.

48. Hedley J refused the application on four grounds:

> "First, given that the parental order is like an adoption order, an order conferring status, there should, so far as is possible, be certainty and clarity and therefore the court in considering such an application should be guided by the authorities on revoking adoption orders. There is no statutory power to do so nor any inherent power other than in the sort of circumstances raised in Re M and Re K. The bar is set very high. Secondly, although the court, Mr. G and SK, were undoubtedly misled by Mrs G in her silence, both as to the affair and her pessimistic perception of the marriage, that, in my judgment, comes nowhere near the circumstances that existed in Re M, which in any event was said should not be used as a precedent on its facts, or in Re K. Thirdly, I do not believe that a revocation of this order is consistent with D's welfare, indeed if anything it conduces against it. This is in sharp contra-distinction to Re M. Mrs G is the only mother that he has known and his welfare will be undermined if she is deposed from that role. Fourthly, I am satisfied that the court would have reached the same decision as it did, even if all the matters revealed in the

> *CAFCASS report had been considered properly by the judge, and I think it more likely than not that such an order would have been made had all the information been disclosed, provided, of course, SK's consent and Mr. G's application had continued."*[5]

49. It is often said that adoption orders are not immune from challenge and therefore the same must be said about parental orders.[6] However this case make it clear that the barrier to revoke a parental order is extremely high and the court will be slow to revoke a parental order.

Conclusion

50. For those embarking on the parental order process, it is important for there to be an understanding of the court's powers and functions and what will be required and expected of applicants. Where there are issues of complexity it is important that they are identified as early as possible and brought to the court's attention. Similarly, in domestic cases, where they might be heard by magistrates or district or circuit judges, the issue of allocation should always be kept under review, so as to prevent any delay (as well as costs) in the proceedings, which will always be contrary to the welfare of the child.

---

5   Per Hedley J at para [43]
6   See *Re B (Adoption Jurisdiction to set aside)* [1995] 2 FLR 1 and *Webster v Norfolk County Council* [2009] 1 FLR 1378

CHAPTER EIGHT
WHAT HAPPENS WHEN THE CRITERIA FOR A PARENTAL ORDER IS NOT MET?

1. In chapter 4 the criteria for a parental order was set out. However, there will be circumstances where it is not possible to obtain a parental order because the applicant(s) do not satisfy the statutory criteria under s54 of the HFEA 2008.

2. Where the criteria is not met, it is likely to be for one of the following reasons:

    a) Domicile cannot be satisfied (n.b. only one of the applicant's must be domiciled in the UK). This will only be a problem where in a joint application **neither** applicant can assert domicile here, or in the case of a single applicant, the single applicant is not domiciled here themselves. This often happens in cases where domicile of origin is elsewhere (or they have lost their domicile in the UK) and have been unable to acquire domicile of choice in this jurisdiction – for example they wish to maintain their 'non-dom' status;

    b) The surrogate does not wish to consent to the making of a parental order;

    c) No biological tie can be established (i.e cases of double gamete donation);

    d) The application is made outside of the 6 month time limit (although, the case of *Re X (a child) (Surrogacy: Time limit)* [2014] EWHC 3135 (Fam) has addressed this issue and if the applicant(s) are able to satisfy certain criteria, an application made outside of the 6 month time limit, should not alone, be a bar to a parental order being granted).

3. It is possible of course that there might be cases where a court refuses to make a parental order where the 'home' or 'enduring family relationship' criteria are not met, but those are less likely given recent cases that have adopted a broad interpretation of their meanings.

4. In cases where consent is the issue between the parties and there is a dispute as to where, and with whom the child should live, the welfare principle will be the court's paramount consideration as to what the ultimate outcome.

5. Where there is deadlock between parties, alternative methods of dispute resolution, such as mediation, should be explored.

6. There are 3 realistic options available where the parental order criteria are not met:

    a) Child arrangements order;

    b) Wardship;

    c) Adoption.

Child arrangements order:

7. By applying for a child arrangements order, an applicant would need the court's permission to apply for such an order as they not automatically qualify to make such an application.

8. Section 10(5) of the Children Act 1989 states:

(5) The following persons are entitled to apply for child arrangements order with respect to a child—

(a) any party to a marriage (whether or not subsisting) in relation to whom the child is a child of the family;

(aa) any civil partner in a civil partnership (whether or not subsisting) in relation to whom the child is a child of the family;

(b) any person with whom the child has lived for a period of at least three years;

(c) any person who—

> *(i) in any case where a child arrangements order in force with respect to the child regulates arrangements relating to with whom the child is to live or when the child is to live with any person, has the consent of each of the persons named in the order as a person with whom the child is to live;*
>
> *(ii) in any case where the child is in the care of a local authority, has the consent of that authority; or*
>
> *(iii) in any other case, has the consent of each of those (if any) who have parental responsibility for the child.*

(d) any person who has parental responsibility for the child by virtue of provision made under section 12(2A).

9. If the surrogate gave consent for the applicants to apply for a child arrangements order, that would satisfy s10(5)(c)(iii). Unless the surrogate is married, there would be no one else that has parental responsibility whose consent would be required.

10. However, if for whatever reason, the surrogate was unable to give consent to applicant(s) applying for a child arrangements order, the court would need to grant leave to the applicant to make that application.

11. When deciding whether or not to grant leave to the applicant to make the application the court is duty bound to have regard to the following factors under s10(9) of the Children Act 1989:

    a) The nature of the proposed application for the section 8 order;

    b) The applicant's connection with the child;

    c) Any risk there might be of that proposed application disrupting the child's life to such an extent that he would be harmed by it; and

    d) Where the child is being looked after by a local authority-

        i. The authority's plans for the child's future; and

        ii. The wishes and feelings of the child's parents.

12. In a case where an applicant is seeking leave, plainly it is only points *a-c* that are engaged when the court applies all of the relevant factors that are contained within the welfare checklist as set out in s1(3) of the Children Act 1989. The nature of the application is an obvious one, and it is an application that will very much advance the welfare of the child. In respect of point c – the nature of the application will have quite the *opposite* effect of disrupting the child's life and it is an order sought to reflect the reality of the child's life currently. In the absence of the court making a child arrangements order (or indeed the court invoking its powers pursuant to the inherent jurisdiction) the child would effectively rendered in a state of legal limbo, all of which should be persuasive factors that would tip the balance to a court granting leave.

13. In *Re A (Foreign surrogacy- Parental responsibility) [2016] EWFC 70* the High Court was concerned with a single male applicant (who was biologically related to the child) who sought a child arrangements order following a surrogacy arrangement in the

USA. The court awarded a child arrangements order that the child live with him, the effect of which is to afford the holder of the child arrangement order with parental responsibility for the child. It is not clear from that judgment whether the court went on to make orders that prohibited the surrogate's ability to exercise her parental responsibility (a 'prohibited steps order). The applicant in that particular case would now satisfy the criteria under S54A of the HFEA 2008, in respect of single applicants, and could apply for a parental order, if the court was satisfied that the court could make an order outside of the 6 month time limit.

14. Where a child arrangements order is used as an alternative to a parental order, in such cases the surrogate will be a respondent to the proceedings.

15. In *H (A child: Surrogacy breakdown) [2017] EWCA Civ 1798* A and B were a male same-sex couple who entered into a surrogacy arrangement with C and D who were a heterosexual married couple. A's sperm and a donor egg resulted in C's pregnancy with H. The parties' relationship broke down subsequently and communication between them ceased. Post birth, C and D informed to A and B to inform them that they no longer wished to follow the terms of the agreement and would not provide their consent to the making of a parental order.

16. At first instance, the matter came before Theis J, where the issues to be determined were where H should live and the amount of contact that should be afforded to the other couple, and whether there should be any restrictions on that couple's ability to exercise parental responsibility. Theis J concluded that the child should live with A and B and made a number of section 8 orders to limit C and D's ability to exercise parental responsibility.

17. C and D appealed, and it was argued on their behalf that at para [22]:

> (1) By limiting their clients' contact and fettering their parental responsibility, the judge had effectively made a parental order in all but name.
>
> (2) The judge should have striven to provide H with two homes and four parents. Instead, she undertook no detailed analysis of the purpose of contact, neglected the Article 8 rights involved, and failed to explain why a level of 'identity contact' that marginalises C and D is necessary or proportionate.
>
> (3) The criticism of C and D for being rigid in wanting their legal child to live with them was unwarranted, and the Judge did not fairly balance it against the undoubted shortcomings of A and B. This imbalance reflected the Judge's treatment of the case as *"a surrogacy gone wrong"*, rather than a case to be approached on normal principles. It led her to adopt a punitive approach towards C and D for having withdrawn from the arrangement.
>
> (4) With reference to the parental involvement presumption at s.1(2A) Children Act 1989, the Judge should have treated the case like any other case of parental breakdown, where separated parents are reminded of the duties, and where the court has powers to support and enforce its orders.
>
> (5) The specific issue orders in relation to the exercise of parental responsibility and travel abroad are too wide and insufficiently precise.

18. The appeal was dismissed, McFarlane LJ, as he then was, making the following observations at the outset of the judgment:

> *(i) Position stated by the Court of Appeal in Re N (a child) [2007] EWCA Civ 1053 was reaffirmed. The essential question in every case is: all things considered, which outcome will be best for the child? The law does not take a special approach to decisions about surrogacy breakdown or other disputes within unconventional family structures. The welfare principle applies with full force in such cases; indeed, the more unusual the facts, the greater the need to keep the child at the heart of the decision, and to ensure that the interests of others prevail only where they are in harmony with the interests of the child.*
>
> *(ii) Although the appeal was trailed as involving novel legal issues about the interface between the Human Fertilisation and Embryology Act 2008 and the Children Act 1989, on examination these issues fell away and the argument ultimately boiled down to the question of whether the Judge erred in her evaluation of the evidence.*
>
> *(iii) The judge rightly took a conventional welfare approach to an unconventional family structure. Her decisions about where the child should live (not appealed) and about the role that should be played by the other family (the focus of this appeal) were ones that she was entitled to reach on the evidence before her.[1]*

19. The overall tenor of the Court of Appeal judgment was that the trial judge was entitled to come to the decision she did having evaluated the evidence and applied the relevant welfare principles.

---

1 Per McFarlane LJ, at para [3]

20. The concluding remarks of the judgment are of note, with the Court of Appeal endorsing Theis J's comments from the first instance judgment, where her ladyship observed:

> *"This case is another example of the complex consequences that can arise from entering into this type of arrangement. Even though C was an experienced surrogate, this case demonstrates the risks involved when parties reach agreement to conceive a child which, if it goes wrong, can cause huge distress to all concerned. For all the adults involved, who all clearly love H, the one thing I know they will agree is that their dispute and this contested litigation has been a harrowing experience for them all. This case is another example of the consequences of not having a properly supported and regulated framework to underpin arrangements of this kind."*[2]

21. Whilst this example is in relation to circumstances of so called 'surrogacy breakdown', the terms of the order could be used to apply to any scenario where the criteria for a parental order is not met with a child arrangements order that provides for:

   a) The child to live with the intended parents, thereby affording them with parental responsibility;

   b) A prohibited steps order that restricts the exercise of the surrogate (and her husband if married)'s parental responsibility without permission of the court;

   c) Provision for the intended parents to exercise their parental responsibility exclusively without the consent of the surrogate (and husband if married);

22. It may also be helpful, particularly in cases where it is by consent, for there to be recitals on the face of any order as follows:

---

2 At para [28]

a) That the child was born as a result of a surrogacy arrangement;

b) If the child was born in a different jurisdiction, a summary of the orders or judicial determinations made in that jurisdiction that grant the intended parent any legal status;

c) Who the child's legal parents are as a matter of English law;

d) Whether the intended parent is genetically related to the child;

e) Whether the surrogate is genetically related to the child;

f) That notwithstanding the surrogate having parental responsibility for the child, she (and her husband if married) agrees to delegate all aspects of parental responsibility to the intended parent(s);

g) Whether, in the event of the death of the intended parents during the child's minority, they have nominated a testamentary guardian to be responsible for the child under *section 5(1)(b) of the Children Act 1989.*

23. Whilst provisions such as these in an order, and the order itself attempt to do the best it can to place the intended parents in the position of legal parents, it does not do so fully as intended parents can only be legal parents by way of an adoption order or a parental order. It means therefore that it is imperative that intended parents seeking to achieve parental status in relation to a child will have to consider taking additional steps in terms of estate planning, for example in relation to inheritance and succession which is not always automatic if they are not legal parents. Similarly, the same issue also arises in relation to citizenship, where specialist immigration advice should be sought.

Wardship

24. Wardship is one of the oldest legal contingencies relating to children and forms part of the inherent jurisdiction of the high court. Its historical origins date back to feudal obligations of the sovereign to protect their subject as *parens patriae* (parent of the country). When a court (it is only a high court judge who has the power to do so) makes a child a 'ward of court' no important step in the child's life can be taken without the court's consent. The court may (as it usually does) vest care and control to a particular person(s) or even to a local authority, but every major decision must be determined by the court.

25. The use of wardship nowadays (i.e. post the 1989 Children Act) is used sparingly, and it does not offer a long-term solution. Circumstances where it is commonly used is in respect of children who are British national who are stranded abroad or abducted to another jurisdiction.

26. In the surrogacy context, wardship was used in the case *M v F & SM (Human Fertilisation and Embryology Act 2008) [2017] EWHC 2176 (Fam)*. Keehan J used wardship as a short-term legal mechanism to secure the placement of a child with the intended mother.

27. In *M v F* the child was carried by a surrogate (SM), however by the time of the child's birth, the child's biological mother (M) and father (F) (i.e their gametes had been used to create the embryo that was transferred to the surrogate) had separated (they were not married). The child's legal parents were the surrogate mother and the biological father. However the biological mother (i.e. the intended mother) had no formal legal status other than being the biological mother, because the person who gives births to the child is always regarded as the child's legal mother, regardless of any biological connection (s33 of the

HFEA 2008)- F did not have parental responsibility for the child: at birth the only person with parental responsibility for the child was the surrogate mother.

28. Immediately post birth, the child was cared for by the biological mother, and she applied for orders under the court's inherent jurisdiction, i.e. wardship. The biological father had indicated from the outset of the proceedings (in a letter he had sent to the court) that he did not wish to be involved in the proceedings, nor involved in the child's upbringing.

29. The child was made a ward of court and the court delegated care and control of the child to the biological mother, with a prohibition that the biological father could not remove the child from the biological mother's care.

30. Whilst it is the least desirable legal framework, there are examples of it being used in surrogacy cases on a long term basis (*JP v LP & Others [2014] EWHC 595 (Fam)*).

31. In *JP v LP* Eleanor King J (as she then was) considered a similar such order appropriate in circumstances where a parental order was not available. The order endorsed by the court in that case provided that:

> *i* The child shall remain a ward of court until further order;
>
> ii A shared residence order as between the mother and father;
>
> iii All issues of parental responsibility are delegated to the mother and father jointly;
>
> iv The surrogate mother is prohibited from exercising her parental responsibility for child without the leave of the court

Adoption

32. Adoption is a possible option where a parental order cannot be granted and has been used in a number of cases. However, adoption is a complex area of law and there are parts of the Adoption and Children Act 2002, which may prevent a parental order being made. However, where it is possible to make an adoption order, it does have the benefit of making the intended parent(s) a legal parent, in the same way that a paranal order does, so it has the key transformative effect in terms of status for the child and the intended parent(s).

33. Where a child has been born as a result of a surrogacy arrangement in another country, and an adoption order is made in that jurisdiction recognising the intended parents as legal parents, it is possible that recognition of that adoption order could be sought in this jurisdiction.

The Adoption (Recognition of Overseas Adoptions) Order 2013 (SI 2013/1801)

34. Chapter 4 of the Adoption and Children Act 2002 is concerned with "The Status of Adopted Children". Section 66 of the Adoption and Children Act 2002, which comes under Chapter 4, sets out the meaning of adoption under chapter 4:

> *[66] Meaning of adoption in Chapter 4*
>
> *(1) In this Chapter "adoption" means*
>
> *a) adoption by an adoption order or a Scottish or Northern Irish adoption order*
>
> *b) adoption by an order made in the Isle of Man or any of the Channel Islands,*

> *c) an adoption effected under the law of a Convention country outside the British Islands, and certified in pursuance of Article 23(1) of the Convention (referred to in this Act as a "Convention adoption"),*
>
> *<u>d) an overseas adoption, or</u>*
>
> *e) an adoption recognised by the law of England and Wales and effected under the law of any other country;*
>
> *and related expressions are to be interpreted accordingly.*

35. Section 67 of the Adoption and Children Act 2002 provides that each and all of these types of adoptions takes effect in English law as if the order had been made by an English court. The order takes effect in England in the same way as an English adoption order – the child is treated in law as if born to the adopters, as their legitimate child and as not being the child of any persons other than the adopters.

36. Section 87 of the ACA 2002 states:

> *87 Overseas adoptions*
>
> *(1) In this Act, "overseas adoption"—*
>
> *(a) means an adoption of a description specified in an order made by the Secretary of State, being a description of adoptions effected under the law of any country or territory outside the British Islands, but*
>
> *(b) does not include a Convention adoption.*

37. What is considered to be an 'overseas adoption' (after 3 January 2014) under s66(1)(d) of the Adoption and Children Act 2002 is governed by a statutory instrument – *The Adoption (Recog-*

nition of Overseas Adoptions) Order 2013 (SI 2013/1801)*. This came into force in England and Wales in January 2014.

38. The key requirement for recognition under the *The Adoption (Recognition of Overseas Adoptions) Order 2013 (SI 2013/1801)* is that he intended parent(s) (i.e. the adoptive parent(s)) must have been habitually resident in England or Wales at the time of the adoption.

39. In terms of procedural steps, the automatic recognition afforded by *The Adoption (Recognition of Overseas Adoptions) Order 2013 (SI 2013/1801)*, means that the intended parents need take no further steps other than to register the adoption with the Office of the Registrar General. Where an intended parent seeks recognition this way Form ACR 53 must be completed.[3]

40. Under English law, 'overseas adoptions' have the same effect as domestic adoptions in terms of the status of the child and the adopters. This means it will have full effect in terms of attribution of parenthood to the adoptive parents, and the termination of all previous parental ties.

Convention adoptions

41. It is possible that recognition of a surrogacy arrangement could be achieved by way of a convention adoption, in circumstances where the child was born abroad. However, this is an even more complex area of family law, and would require specialist advice.

---

3   https://assets.publishing.service.gov.uk/government/uploads/system/uploads/attachment_data/file/832597/1_ACR_52_June_2019.v1.pdf

Cases where adoption orders have been made following a surrogacy arrangement

42. *B v C (Surrogacy – Adoption) [2015] EWFC 17* concerned an application for an adoption order in respect of a child by his biological father, where the father had entered into a surrogacy arrangement where his mother was a gestational surrogate (i.e. a donor egg was used). Theis J awarded an adoption order to the single intended parent.

43. Dealing with the relevant legal framework, Theis J sets out the provisions of the HFEA 2008 that affords legal parentage to the gestational surrogate s33(1) and her husband s35(1). The provisions of s54(2) (application by two people) at the time prevented the intended father from being able to apply for a parental order. However, the court was satisfied that under the provisions of the Adoption and Children Act 2002, it was lawful and, in the child's, best interests that an adoption order was made.

44. An interesting feature of the case was that since the intended father was treated in law as a relative of the child (i.e. his legal brother), no criminal offence was committed in the child being placed for adoption with his intended father. Section 92 of the Adoption and Children Act 2002 states:

> "(1) A person who is neither an adoption agency nor acting in pursuance of an order of the High Court must not take any of the steps mentioned in subsection (2).
>
> (2) The steps are—
>
>> (a) asking a person other than an adoption agency to provide a child for adoption,

>   (b) asking a person other than an adoption agency to provide prospective adopters for a child,
>
>   (c) offering to find a child for adoption,
>
>   (d) offering a child for adoption to a person other than an adoption agency,
>
>   (e) handing over a child to any person other than an adoption agency with a view to the child's adoption by that or another person,
>
>   (f) receiving a child handed over to him in contravention of paragraph (e),
>
>   (g) entering into an agreement with any person for the adoption of a child, or for the purpose of facilitating the adoption of a child, where no adoption agency is acting on behalf of the child in the adoption,
>
>   (h) initiating or taking part in negotiations of which the purpose is the conclusion of an agreement within paragraph (g),
>
>   (i) causing another person to take any of the steps mentioned in paragraphs (a) to (h).
>
> (3) Subsection (1) does not apply to a person taking any of the steps mentioned in paragraphs (d), (e), (g), (h) and (i) of subsection (2) if the following condition is met.
>
> (4) The condition is that—
>
>   (a) the prospective adopters are parents, relatives or guardians of the child (or one of them is), or

(b) the prospective adopter is the partner of a parent of the child."

45. Breach of s92 is a criminal offence under s93 of the Adoption and Children Act 2002. As Theis J observed:

> *"32. What this case highlights, is that but for the close familial relationship between B and C, their actions would have breached these important statutory provisions and potentially left them liable to a criminal prosecution under both s.93 ACA 2002 and s.70 CA 1989.*
>
> *33. It is therefore imperative that single parents contemplating parenthood through surrogacy obtain comprehensive legal advice as to how to proceed as adoption is the only means to ensure that they are the only legal parents of their child. The process under which they can achieve this is a legal minefield, they need to ensure that all the appropriate steps are undertaken to secure lifelong legal security regarding their status with the child."*[4]

46. Plainly the facts of this case are unique and it will be rare for a case to have similar facts. In any event, the intended father in *B v C*, on the facts of the case would now qualify for a parental order as a single applicant under S54A of the HFEA 2008 and so it would not be necessary for the court and the parties to deploy this kind of legal creativity.

47. *B (Adoption: Surrogacy and Parental Responsibility) [2018] EWFC 86* concerned an application for an adoption order by a single applicant, X, who had entered into a surrogacy arrangement with her husband, Y, in the Ukraine. Having identified a gestational surrogate, Z, in the Ukraine, an embryo transfer took place using a donor egg and the intended father's

---

4   Per Theis J at para [32]-[33]

sperm. Prior to the child being born in August 2017, the intended parents separated and the intended father later indicated that he did not wish to play a role in the child's life. After returning to this jurisdiction post birth (having encountered difficulties with the child's immigration status), X was obliged to bring the matter to court for urgent directions when the child required medical treatment and X required parental responsibility to give valid consent.

48. The matter retuned to court and Theis J made a child arrangements order that the child live with X (having granted permission for X to apply for such an order) thereby affording parental responsibility to X. The child, B, was joined as a party to the proceedings and X later indicated her intention to apply for an adoption order in respect of B. Whilst Y, the biological father, had played no role in the proceedings, the court directed that he be given notice of the adoption application, and Z, the gestational surrogate, was joined as a party to the adoption application. The adoption application was supported by the child's guardian and Z the gestational surrogate.

49. In making an adoption order, the court considered the lifelong welfare needs of the child (i.e. the welfare checklist under s1(4) of the Adoption and Children Act 2002) and concluded that *"B's welfare requires Z's consent to be dispensed with. Z has been consistent in expressing her wish to have no further involvement in B's life. B needs the security and stability an adoption order will give her, securing her relationship with X long term."*[5]

50. Whilst Theis J doesn't deal directly with section 95 of the Adoption and Children Act 2002 (prohibition of certain payments), the key point to be taken from this case is that the intended mother had entered into a surrogacy arrangement expecting to become the child's legal parent by applying for a

---

5   Per Theis J at para [83]

parental order with her husband, however it was the subsequent separation of the intended parents during the surrogacy process which prevented the surrogate from applying for a parental order.

Conclusion

51. It will be important to identify cases where a parental order is not possible at an early stage, ideally before a surrogacy arrangement takes place. Where it is identified, it can ensure that swift action is taken post birth to ensure that the primary carers of the child have some form of legal status and are able to exercise parental responsibility.

52. In cases where there has been a breakdown in relationship between the intended parent(s) and the surrogate, welfare will be the court's number one guiding principle as to where the child should live. However, mediation should be encouraged where possible if deemed appropriate.

CHAPTER NINE
CONCLUDING COMMENTS

1. Surrogacy remains a complex area of law. The often-sad reality of cases that find themselves in the law reports are the cases where advice early on would have no doubt assisted and possibly reduced the scope of litigation. There are, sadly, many cases that open with "this case is yet another cautionary tale".

2. As Theis J observed in *CC v DD [2014] EWHC 1307 (Fam)* in a case concerning an international surrogacy arrangement: "*This case highlights once more the legal complexities in this area of the law and the need for those who embark on international surrogacy arrangements to ensure they have expert advice both here and in the jurisdiction where the arrangement is taking place.*"[1]

3. The absence of any regulation in this jurisdiction means that there are areas where uncertainty is prevalent. For example, the confusion over what amounts to reasonable expenses. Legal representatives are also left with some uncertainty, being unaware of the extent to which they are able to provide advice without falling foul of the Surrogacy Arrangements Act 1985.

Practical guidance before entering a surrogacy arrangement

4. For intended parents thinking about surrogacy, the first question they must ask themselves more generally is in what country do they wish to undertake a surrogacy arrangement. Whatever country that is decided, the key point is that intended parents must take responsibility for undertaking their own due diligence. This is particularly the case when the arrangement

---

1   Per Theis J at para [3]

takes place in another jurisdiction, and even more so if it is a jurisdiction where surrogacy might be viewed of as a new emerging market compared to surrogacy arrangements in jurisdictions where the courts routinely make parental orders. Where intended parents are expected to have limited contact with a surrogate, it should raise a number of questions to intended parents (e.g. is the surrogate fully aware what she is agreeing to take part in?)

5. The following are just a few suggestions of the types of issues that should be considered *before* intended parents embark on entering a surrogacy arrangement and certainly before they embark on any form of medical treatment.

   a) What are the relevant surrogacy laws in the country where the surrogacy arrangement is due to take place and where the child is to be born?

   b) Will the intended parents be recognised as parents in that country?

   c) What is the surrogate's status at birth?

   d) What is the surrogate's spouse's status at birth?

   e) What legal steps need to be taken to secure legal recognition in that county if it is not automatic, either during the pregnancy (e.g. pre-birth orders) or post birth?

   f) If an agency is involved, what role do they play in matching the surrogate with intended parents?

   g) How much contact is permitted with the surrogate - i.e. is it an 'at arm's length' relationship or are the intended parents permitted and encouraged to have a relationship with the surrogate?

h) What relationship, if any, is to take place post birth between the surrogate and the child? Is there agreement in respect of those issues?

i) What steps need to be taken to get back to the UK?

j) Is it possible to obtain travel documentation for the child?

k) What nationality will the child have at birth?

6. In international cases, it would be prudent to have legal representation identified at an early stage to assist in the process of acquiring status in that jurisdiction. Where issues of potential complexity are identified, it is not uncommon for legal teams in both jurisdictions to discuss issues, particularly where it may be of assistance for a legal representative in another jurisdiction to have knowledge of what the process is in this jurisdiction to obtain a parental order.

7. It goes without saying that record keeping is essential. It is imperative that all who embark on a surrogacy arrangement keep accurate and up to date records concerning the surrogacy before, during and after the surrogacy (up to the point of a parental order being made), particularly in relation to expenses. In international cases where agencies are involved they often have a ledger, which sets out sums that have been deducted and for what purpose, but it is also important that intended parents understand what money is being used for.

8. In terms of nationality and immigration issues, expert legal advice should always be sought. Even in cases where one or both of the intended parents have British, nationality, it does not automatically mean that the child will be British at the time of birth. The circumstances of the surrogacy may dictate how nationality is acquired. The general rule is that a child who is the subject of a parental order made in a UK court after 6 April 2010 will become a British citizen from the date of the order if

either one of the persons who obtained the order is a British citizen. The Home Office guidance (March 2019) on nationality in surrogacy cases should be considered.[2]

9. In cases where a child is born outside of the UK and has a British legal parent, the child will usually be considered British by descent (prior to a parental order being made). Thus, in cases where surrogate is not married and the British intended father's gametes were used, the intended father would be a legal parent, and it may well be possible to obtain a British travel documentation prior to a parental order being made with appropriate DNA paternity testing. Obviously, that only relates to the intended father, because even if the gametes of an intended mother were used, the legal parent will be the surrogate and the process may take a little longer.

10. At the time of writing, there is no Home Office approved country list for surrogacy cases, equivalent to *The Adoption (Recognition of Overseas Adoptions) Order 2013*. As discussed in earlier chapters, adoption list contains a number of countries where the Home Office, states where an adoption order has made overseas, that the adoption is afforded automatic recognition here subject to particular criteria being satisfied and documentary evidence being supplied to the Office of the Registrar General.

11. It is hoped this book is a useful to those embarking on surrogacy arrangements. It is not intended to alarm prospective parents, but more to highlight to would-be intended parents and their legal advisers the steps they need to be taken to facilitate a smooth process to acquiring parenthood.

---

2 https://assets.publishing.service.gov.uk/government/uploads/system/uploads/attachment_data/file/787212/nationality-policy-surrogacy-v2.0ext.pdf

12. However, given the complexity of the subject matter and the likelihood for law reform, certainly at some point this decade, individuals should ensure they are kept up to date with any new legislative changes to the legal framework for surrogacy in this jurisdiction.

MORE BOOKS BY LAW BRIEF PUBLISHING

A selection of our other titles available now:-

'Covid-19, Homeworking and the Law – The Essential Guide to Employment and GDPR Issues' by Forbes Solicitors
'Covid-19, Force Majeure and Frustration of Contracts – The Essential Guide' by Keith Markham
'Covid-19 and Criminal Law – The Essential Guide' by Ramya Nagesh
'Covid-19 and Family Law in England and Wales – The Essential Guide' by Safda Mahmood
'Covid-19 and the Implications for Planning Law – The Essential Guide' by Bob Mc Geady & Meyric Lewis
'Covid-19, Residential Property, Equity Release and Enfranchisement – The Essential Guide' by Paul Sams and Louise Uphill
'Covid-19, Brexit and the Law of Commercial Leases – The Essential Guide' by Mark Shelton
'Covid-19 and the Law Relating to Food in the UK and Republic of Ireland – The Essential Guide' by Ian Thomas
'A Practical Guide to the General Data Protection Regulation (GDPR) – 2nd Edition' by Keith Markham
'Ellis on Credit Hire – Sixth Edition' by Aidan Ellis & Tim Kevan
'A Practical Guide to Working with Litigants in Person and McKenzie Friends in Family Cases' by Stuart Barlow
'Protecting Unregistered Brands: A Practical Guide to the Law of Passing Off' by Lorna Brazell
'A Practical Guide to Secondary Liability and Joint Enterprise Post-Jogee' by Joanne Cecil & James Mehigan

'A Practical Guide to the Pre-Action RTA Claims Protocol for Personal Injury Lawyers' by Antonia Ford
'A Practical Guide to Neighbour Disputes and the Law' by Alexander Walsh
'A Practical Guide to Forfeiture of Leases' by Mark Shelton
'A Practical Guide to Coercive Control for Legal Practitioners and Victims' by Rachel Horman
'A Practical Guide to Rights Over Airspace and Subsoil' by Daniel Gatty
'Tackling Disclosure in the Criminal Courts – A Practitioner's Guide' by Narita Bahra QC & Don Ramble
'A Practical Guide to the Law of Driverless Cars – Second Edition' by Alex Glassbrook, Emma Northey & Scarlett Milligan
'A Practical Guide to TOLATA Claims' by Greg Williams
'Artificial Intelligence – The Practical Legal Issues' by John Buyers
'A Practical Guide to the Law of Prescription in Scotland' by Andrew Foyle
'A Practical Guide to the Construction and Rectification of Wills and Trust Instruments' by Edward Hewitt
'A Practical Guide to the Law of Bullying and Harassment in the Workplace' by Philip Hyland
'How to Be a Freelance Solicitor: A Practical Guide to the SRA-Regulated Freelance Solicitor Model' by Paul Bennett
'A Practical Guide to Prison Injury Claims' by Malcolm Johnson
'A Practical Guide to the Small Claims Track' by Dominic Bright
'A Practical Guide to Advising Clients at the Police Station' by Colin Stephen McKeown-Beaumont
'A Practical Guide to Antisocial Behaviour Injunctions' by Iain Wightwick
'Practical Mediation: A Guide for Mediators, Advocates, Advisers, Lawyers, and Students in Civil, Commercial, Business, Property, Workplace, and Employment Cases' by Jonathan Dingle with John Sephton
'The Mini-Pupillage Workbook' by David Boyle

'A Practical Guide to Crofting Law' by Brian Inkster
'A Practical Guide to Spousal Maintenance' by Liz Cowell
'A Practical Guide to the Law of Domain Names and Cybersquatting' by Andrew Clemson
'A Practical Guide to the Law of Gender Pay Gap Reporting' by Harini Iyengar
'A Practical Guide to the Rights of Grandparents in Children Proceedings' by Stuart Barlow
'NHS Whistleblowing and the Law' by Joseph England
'Employment Law and the Gig Economy' by Nigel Mackay & Annie Powell
'A Practical Guide to Noise Induced Hearing Loss (NIHL) Claims' by Andrew Mckie, Ian Skeate, Gareth McAloon
'An Introduction to Beauty Negligence Claims – A Practical Guide for the Personal Injury Practitioner' by Greg Almond
'Intercompany Agreements for Transfer Pricing Compliance' by Paul Sutton
'Zen and the Art of Mediation' by Martin Plowman
'A Practical Guide to the SRA Principles, Individual and Law Firm Codes of Conduct 2019 – What Every Law Firm Needs to Know' by Paul Bennett
'A Practical Guide to Adoption for Family Lawyers' by Graham Pegg
'A Practical Guide to Industrial Disease Claims' by Andrew Mckie & Ian Skeate
'A Practical Guide to Redundancy' by Philip Hyland
'A Practical Guide to Vicarious Liability' by Mariel Irvine
'A Practical Guide to Applications for Landlord's Consent and Variation of Leases' by Mark Shelton
'A Practical Guide to Relief from Sanctions Post-Mitchell and Denton' by Peter Causton
'A Practical Guide to Equity Release for Advisors' by Paul Sams
'A Practical Guide to Unlawful Eviction and Harassment' by Stephanie Lovegrove
'A Practical Guide to the Law Relating to Food' by Ian Thomas

'A Practical Guide to Financial Services Claims' by Chris Hegarty
'The Law of Houses in Multiple Occupation: A Practical Guide to HMO Proceedings' by Julian Hunt
'A Practical Guide to Unlawful Eviction and Harassment' by Stephanie Lovegrove
'A Practical Guide to Solicitor and Client Costs' by Robin Dunne
'Occupiers, Highways and Defective Premises Claims: A Practical Guide Post-Jackson – 2nd Edition' by Andrew Mckie
'A Practical Guide to Financial Ombudsman Service Claims' by Adam Temple & Robert Scrivenor
'A Practical Guide to Advising Schools on Employment Law' by Jonathan Holden
'A Practical Guide to Running Housing Disrepair and Cavity Wall Claims: 2nd Edition' by Andrew Mckie & Ian Skeate
'A Practical Guide to Holiday Sickness Claims – 2nd Edition' by Andrew Mckie & Ian Skeate
'Arguments and Tactics for Personal Injury and Clinical Negligence Claims' by Dorian Williams
'A Practical Guide to QOCS and Fundamental Dishonesty' by James Bentley
'A Practical Guide to Drone Law' by Rufus Ballaster, Andrew Firman, Eleanor Clot
'A Practical Guide to Compliance for Personal Injury Firms Working With Claims Management Companies' by Paul Bennett
'A Practical Guide to the Landlord and Tenant Act 1954: Commercial Tenancies' by Richard Hayes & David Sawtell
'A Practical Guide to Dog Law for Owners and Others' by Andrea Pitt
'RTA Allegations of Fraud in a Post-Jackson Era: The Handbook – 2nd Edition' by Andrew Mckie
'RTA Personal Injury Claims: A Practical Guide Post-Jackson' by Andrew Mckie
'On Experts: CPR35 for Lawyers and Experts' by David Boyle
'An Introduction to Personal Injury Law' by David Boyle

'A Practical Guide to Chronic Pain Claims' by Pankaj Madan
'A Practical Guide to Claims Arising from Fatal Accidents' by James Patience
'A Practical Guide to Subtle Brain Injury Claims' by Pankaj Madan

These books and more are available to order online direct from the publisher at www.lawbriefpublishing.com, where you can also read free sample chapters. For any queries, contact us on 0844 587 2383 or mail@lawbriefpublishing.com.

Our books are also usually in stock at www.amazon.co.uk with free next day delivery for Prime members, and at good legal bookshops such as Wildy & Sons.

We are regularly launching new books in our series of practical day-to-day practitioners' guides. Visit our website and join our free newsletter to be kept informed and to receive special offers, free chapters, etc.

You can also follow us on Twitter at www.twitter.com/lawbriefpub.

www.ingramcontent.com/pod-product-compliance
Ingram Content Group UK Ltd.
Pitfield, Milton Keynes, MK11 3LW, UK
UKHW021509101125
8875UKWH00016B/218